Stephen Darby

Place and Field Names, Cookham Parish, Berks

Stephen Darby

Place and Field Names, Cookham Parish, Berks

ISBN/EAN: 9783744763851

Printed in Europe, USA, Canada, Australia, Japan

Cover: Foto ©ninafisch / pixelio.de

More available books at **www.hansebooks.com**

PLACE AND FIELD NAMES,

COOKHAM PARISH,

BERKS.

BY

STEPHEN DARBY.

FOR PRIVATE CIRCULATION.

1899.

INTRODUCTION.

A very great change in the aspect of Cookham Parish was effected about the year 1845 by the enclosure of the large open Common Fields under the Common Fields Enclosure Act; and, sanctioned by the same Act of Parliament, exchanges were effected which resulted in the removal of many old boundaries, and a readjustment of field divisions. With this readjustment there disappeared a number of names; or, if these were retained, it was often under conditions by which they were robbed of their significance.

As field and place names afford from time to time to a certain extent a history of the locality, it seemed worth the pains to perpetuate those which the enclosure had silenced by giving their place on the Parish Ordnance Map. This was made the easier from the fact that some few years prior to the enclosure a survey of the Parish had been made for the purposes of the Tithe Commutation, which afforded not only a list of names then in use, but showed their actual location on the Map or Plan prepared at the same time. (With but two or three exceptions, names adopted since that time have not been noticed.)

This was the first and chief object; but in the second place there seemed to be some interest in ascertaining which amongst these names, either as modernised words or corruptions of the old names, could be traceable to such as were in use in earlier times.

A survey of the manor made in the year 1609 for King James I. greatly helped in this; and, compared with the more recent list, shows the changes of names which had occurred between the commencement of the seventeenth and the middle of the nineteenth centuries. With the means now available, the sites to which many of the old names belonged are not traceable ; but the names have been given with the dates of their occurrence and how they appeared ; unless it be in the 1609 survey, when this last is omitted.

It is interesting to note that whilst a large number of place names are acquired from those of owners or occupiers, yet in the earlier times these owners or occupiers had gained their names from the places. And so one is led on in the third instance to try and ascertain the origin of these place names.

The localising on the Ordnance Map the names in use at the time of the Tithe Commutation Survey is, I trust, fairly accurate, and so I believe is the connection between old and new names.

For the derivation of the names I am, with a few exceptions, indebted to ' Words and Places,' by the Rev. Isaac Taylor, and to ' Traces of History in the Names of Places,' by Flavell Edmunds ; more especially to the latter work. As to the correctness of my conclusions there will, no doubt, be differences of opinion. For recording any such criticisms or for corrections and additions there are added a few blank leaves ; and if, as it is hoped, these be made use of, one object for printing this record will have been effected.

Old deeds of property in the possession of many would probably yield both a number of fresh names, and afford a clue to the locality of some of the old names that are yet unplaced.

S. D.

Cookham Dean;
January, 1899.

ABBREVIATIONS.

T. M. NO.   Number of plot on the Tithe Map of the year 1845.

O. M. NO.   Number of plot on the 25-inch Parish Ordnance Survey Map of Cookham Parish.

C. C. R.   Cookham Manor Court Rolls.

Cookham Wills.   From the Court of the Archdeacon of Berkshire, Somerset House Records.

Maid. Corp. Rec.   From the Maidenhead Corporation Records extracted by the Rev. Mr. Gorham.

A.D. 1609.   A survey, taken this year, of the Cookham Manor property.

Com. Survey.   A survey, taken in the year 1650, of the Cookham Manor property, by the Parliamentarian Commission.

Taylor.   ' Words and Places,' by the Rev. Isaac Taylor.

Edm.   ' Traces of History in the Names of Places,' by Flavell Edmunds.

    "   *B.* British word.

    "   *C.* Celtic word.

    "   *D.* Danish word.

    "   *E.* Anglo-Saxon word.

    "   *L.* Latin word.

    "   *N.* Norse word.

    "   *N. F.* Norman-French word.

ALDEBURY. A.D. 1324. Messuage in Cocham granted to John le Spencer called Aldebury. (Inq. qd. damn.) *See* North Moor.

Probably called Aldebury, or sometimes Oldebury, in contra-distinction to the Cookham village Bury, which is sometimes styled the Viccaridge Berry. *See* The Berrys.

A.D. 1415. William Louch bequeaths land at Oldebury. (COOKHAM WILLS).

Ald from *cald*, old, and Burgh or Bury, *E.*, from "*burg*," a fortification (Edm.).

ALEXANDERS. A.D. 1509. Land at Hoo called Alexanders (C. C. R.).

ALMSHOUSE CLOSE. TITHE MAP, NO. 2325.7 ; ORDNANCE MAP, NO. 249 (part of). Adjoining the almshouses belonging to the Salters' Company.

ALVILLE HATCHE. A.D. 1680. John Sawyer and his son were killed by lightning at Alville Hatche (COOKHAM CHURCH REGISTER). Francis Dell, a labourer, passing that way, found the farmer, his son, and four horses dead.

A detailed account of the disaster was published at the time, in a broadside, by John Harding, at the "Bible and Anchor" in Newport Street, near Leicester Fields, London.

Alville or Eldfield Hatche was situated at the upper part of Nightingale Place, or between that and Cookham Rise.

Alville is a corruption of Eldfield. Hatche, Haches,

E., from *hæca*, a bar (Edm.). Hatch, a hitchgate ; the French *hèche* (Taylor).

ANDRESHAMS. A.D. 1536. "Lionel Norris grants Humphrey Cheyney reversion of Andreshams (C. C. R.).

APS MEAD. A.D. 1609. To John Reading, formerly to Babham.

Eps, *E.*, from *æps*, aspen tree.

In 1696 Thomas Savage paid, for an aid, for Aps Mead 9*s*. 9*d*. John Savage at the same time paid on a part of Babham.

Aps Mead was probably near to Bartle Mead, or Slowgrove.

ARCHERY BUTTS. A.D. 1509. "The Tithing man presents that there are no Archery Butts ; and the inhabitants are ordered to provide them under a penalty " (C. C. R.).

ASSHEHEIT. A.D. 1634. An island in the river Thames " of which Sir Henry Guildford claims to be seised " (Exch. Ct. Enq.).

ASSONS. A.D. 1697. The " Saracen's Head " property, Maidenhead, is appointed Reeve for Assons.

BABHAM'S END. The ancient family of Babham were the owners for several centuries. The land of Babham's End extended on the south to the ford in the river Thames where the old highway crossed it. Did the Babhams derive their name from the property, " Babba-ham," or were they descendants of an old Saxon family ? Babba was a widely spread Saxon name and a chief's name. *See* Babham's Inn.

BABHAM'S INN. T. M. NO. 395 ; O. M. NO. 459. *See* **Babham's End.**

BABHAM'S LEE. A.D. 1634. "The three streams join between Page's Wharf and Babham's Lee " (Depons. Exch. Ct.).

BACK LANE, COOKHAM. From Cookham Moor to the Sutton Road. A portion of this is raised or causewayed. Until the New Road was made in 1836, the Back Lane continued with a bend until it reached the village street where the chapel now is.

BACK LANE, MAIDENHEAD. Now called West Street. It connects the Cookham and Marlow roads. At some thirty yards from the Cookham road it was crossed by the old roadway from Braywick to Cockmarsh, described by the Rev. Mr. Kerry in his ' History of Bray.'

BALD STEYS, or PEAKED BALD STEYS. T. M. NO. 1501; O. M. NO. 777 (part of). It is a part of Highway Farm.

BARDEL DOWN. A.D. 1609. A part of Pinkneys. The name is acquired from a former owner. *See* Pinkneys Hill.

BARDOLFS. A.D. 1609. Belonged together with Pinkneys to Thomas Waller.

Bardolfs was a small manor, probably within the manor of Pinkneys. It belonged A.D. 1432 to Sir Thomas Bardolf, Knt.

Bardolfs now forms a part of Great Bartley.

BARE LEAZE. A.D. 1561. A Close called Bare Leaze, belonging to Arthur Babham (C. C. R.).

BARLEY CLOSE. A.D. 1609. A part of Lawrences, belonging to the Canons of Windsor. Now a portion of John's Close.

Barley is probably a corruption of Bardolf.

BARN CLOSE. A.D. 1609. Part of Bullox. *See* Barn Close, White Place.

BARN CLOSE. Spencers. T. M. NO. 1236; O. M. NO. 615.

BARN CLOSE. White Place. T. M. NO. 462; O. M. NO. 495.

BARN CLOSE. Winter Hill. T. M. NO. 189; O. M. NO. 136.

BARN PARK. A.D. 1609. Near to Maidenhead, in the possession of Richard Austin.

BARN STITCH. T. M. NO. 179 ; O. M. NO. 164 (a part of). *See* Stich.

BARNEY, GREAT and LITTLE. T. M. NOS. 1196, 1197 ; O. M. NO. 678.

BARNEY HEDGE SHOT. T. M. NO. 1808; O. M. NO. 22.

BARRETT FERE. A.D. 1609. A part of Pinkneys.

BARTLE MEAD. A.D. 1609. It contained 51½ acres amongst nineteen owners.

The name Bartle Mead is no doubt a corruption of Bartholomew, and acquired from some custom formerly observed on that saint's day. It was a Lammas meadow held in severalty for the hay crop, and in common of pasturage by the owners during the remainder of the year..

A.D. 1523. It is reported that a ditch through Bartelmede and a highway from Bartelmede are obstructed (C. C. R.).

A.D. 1609. Survey of the manor, it is written Bartle Meade.

A.D. 1617. In a deed of settlement, Cutler and wife, it is written Bartle Mead (private doc.).

A.D. 1640. Sir E. Mansfield to find labourers to mow the King's grass in the King's meadow called Bartle Meade.

A.D. 1643. Sir E. Mansfield had 25 acres 1 swathe in Bartle Meade.

A.D. 1650. Sir E. Mansfield is freeholder of a meadow in Bartle Meade. Withbrook is bounded on the east by Bartle Meade (Commonwealth Survey).

A.D. 1650. Survey of ground known as the Marsh, and Battlinge Mead (Commonwealth Survey).

A.D. 1673. Land owned by the Crown in Bratlinge Mead (C. C. R.).

A.D. 1704. Environed by a common meadow called Bartle Mead.

A.D. 1706. John Hamerton sells John Dodson half an acre of meadow in Bartle Mead (private doc.).

In the Ordnance Map the name is now changed from Bartle Mead to Batlynge Mead, which is said to be the traditional site of a battle between the Saxons and Danes. Is not this tradition a modern invention? *See* Bartle Mead.

BARTLE MEAD. T. M. NOS. 1049–88 ; O. M. NO. 662. At the time of the enclosure it measured fifty acres amongst twenty-seven owners.

A mound in Bartle Mead supposed to be a very ancient tumulus, when examined in the year 1883 by Dr. Stevens and Mr. Rutland, yielded remains of articles for domestic use, which proved to be no earlier than the fourteenth century, and having no connection with either Saxon or Danes.

The adjoining meadow, O. M. NO. 498, is the supposed site of a battle between the Royalists and Parliamentarians, and cannon balls (or a cannon ball) of that period having been unearthed at White Place affords some ground for the tradition. The roadway, which not many years before this had been the highway from London to Oxford, crossed the river by a ford at this spot. It is noticeable that it is in the Commonwealth Survey only that the name Battlinge appears. *See* **BARTLE MEAD.**

BARTLEY, GREAT. T. M. NO. 1389 ; O. M. NO. 768.

BASSES. A.D. 1609. Owned by Warner.

A.D. 1356. Messuage and half a virgate of land belonging to Peter le Basset (C. C. R.). This is possibly partly Bishops Orchard, now Park House. *See* Bishops Orchard.

BASSETS. A.D. 1706. Richard Lee was Reeve and Collector for Bassets.

BASSE MEAD. A.D. 1609. A common meadow, in area 8½ acres, amongst seven owners.

Basse Mead, or Rushy Mead. Bailey, in his Dictionary, gives " Bass—a collar made of rushes." For centuries rushes were used very largely for domestic purposes, and until quite recent years we had bass brooms and rush lights. *See* Bass Mead.

BASS MEAD. T. M. NOS. 634–49 ; O. M. NOS. 374–82. An area of eight acres amongst thirteen owners. It was severalled for haytime, and held by the joint owners in common of pasturage during the remainder of the year. It is a low-lying piece of ground yielding rushes, but not abundantly, as it would have in former years when not so well drained. *See* **BASSE MEAD.**

BASS MEAD SHOT. T. M. NOS. 587 and 606 ; O. M. NO. 373.

BASSE MEAD CLOSE. A.D. 1633. Holderness conveys to Godfrey "a Close known as Basse Mead Close " (private doc.).

BATTLINGE MEAD. *See* Bartle Mead.

BAYLLS. A.D. 1609. It belonged to Godfrey. A.D. 1552. It appears in the will of Robert Kember. Prior to that it was the property of Lord Sandes, Chancellor to Henry VIII (Kerry's Bray). It was situate in some part of Maidenhead.

BEANLEAZE. A.D. 1634. " A meadow divided from Shawses by the stream " (Enq. Ex. Ct.). So that it would have been a part of Odney. Bare Leaze ?

BEECHEN GROVE. A.D. 1609. Belonged to Weldon. *See* Beechen Grove, Cannon Court.

BEECHEN GROVE CLOSE. A.D. 1609. Part of the Manor of Pinkneys. *See* Beeching Grove, Pinkneys.

BEECHEN GROVE WOOD. A.D. 1609. Part of the Manor of Pinkneys. *See* Beeching Grove, Pinkneys.

BEECHEN GROVE WOOD. A.D. 1609. Belonged to Weldon. *See* Beechen Grove, Cannon Court.

BEECHEN GROVE, CANNON COURT. T. M. NO. 1300 ; O. M. NO. 514.

BEECHING GROVE, PINKNEYS. T. M. NO. 1378 ; O. M. NO. 635.

BEGGAR'S SHAW. T. M. NO. 80 ; O. M. NO. 120 (part of). Would Beggars be a corruption of big house ?

BELL ACRE. T. M. NO. 610 ; O. M. NO. 386 (part of).

BELTON'S BARN. A.D. 1609. Belonged to Prymer. A.D. 1650. "Hugh Louiesy paid 2s. rent for biltons barne" (Commonwealth Survey).

BERENDEMULLE. A.D. 1329. "Assart lands enclosed in the Manor and Vill of Cokham at Berendemulle" (Pat. Rolls, 2 Ed. 3rd).

BERRY. A.D. 1609. Bury, Burgh, *E.*, from *burg*, a fortification (Edm.). From the Anglo-Saxon *burh* or *byrig*, an earthwork (Taylor). *See* The Berrys.

BERRYS, THE. T. M. NO. 235 ; O. M. NO. 195. The ground in this enclosure lies higher than most of that surrounding it. *See* Viccaridge Berry.

BIGFRITH. A.D. 1609. "An open wood and common ; by estimation 200 acres, well set with young beech, which the tenants preserve in their own right." A.D. 1321. Bigfrith occurs in an Inq. ad quod damn. held 14 Ed. 2nd.
   Frith *B*, said by Camden to be a wood (Edm.). Frith, a wood, occurs in Chaucer (Bailey). Frith, Saxon "peace," signifies a wood held to be sacred and a sanctuary ; thus its distinction from Hurst and Holt (Bailey).

BIGFRITH, GREAT. A.D. 1650. Area 100 acres.

BIGFRITH, LITTLE. A.D. 1650. Area 50 acres. "The wood of which has wasted and long ago disappeared" (Commonwealth Survey).

BIGFRITH CLOSE. A.D. 1609. Belonging to Wood-mancutts. *See* Bigfrith Close.

BIGFRITH CLOSE. T. M. NO. 963 ; O. M. NO. 253.

BIGFRITH SHAW. T. M. NO. 971 ; O. M. NO. 257 (part of).
Formerly Till Close and Long Close.

BIRDS CLOSE. T. M. NO. 353 ; O. M. NO. 421 (part of).
Named from some former owner or occupier. The Birds were at an earlier period somewhat numerous in the Parish.
A.D. 1663. William Bird collects land tax.
A.D. 1696. William Bird is assessed to land tax at £3.
A.D. 1672. Ralph Bird is one of the Widbrook Trustees appointed by Queen Elizabeth.

BISHOPS ORCHARD. T. M. NO. 596 ; O. M. NO. 370.
The name acquired from a former occupant, viz. Bishop, who was keeper on the manor and lived here at the beginning of this century.

BISHOPS SHOT. T. M. NO. 650 ; O. M. NO. 366. Part of Ham Field.

BLACK BOTTES. A.D. 1524. "John Kent has made a way at Black Bottes" (C. C. R. ; *see* Black Butts).

BLACK BUTTS. T. M. NOS. 284 and 565 ; O. M. NO. 441. A piece of ground by the side of the high-way from Cookham Moor to the Sutton Road. It was probably the old archery ground.

BLACK BUTTS FURLONG. T. M. NOS. 482 to 567 ; O. M. NO. 468. A part of Sutton Field.

BLACKAMORE LANE. The road from North Town fields to the Ray.

BLACKAMORE MEADOW. T. M. NO. 1997 ; O. M. NOS. 94, 127, 128, 132, 133.

BLACKMOORE LANE. A.D. 1609. A close of land, part of Saracen's Head property, called Blackmoore Lane. The name comes, probably, from the Blakemore family.

A.D. 1438. John Blakemore appears as a witness (C. C. R.).

A.D. 1440. William Blakemore appears as a witness (C. C. R.).

A.D. 1530. John Ashby holds half a hide of land called William Blacmors.

A.D. 1576. Andrew Blackmore held land in Holman Lease.

BLAKEMORE. A.D. 1477. "Ditch uncovered at Blakemore" (C. C. R.).

BOKELAND. A.D. 1483. "Bokeland, otherwise Pinkney" (C. C. R.).

BOLTERS LOCK CLOSE. A.D. 1609. Portion of John Turner's property: probably a part of Lock Mead.

BORROWLAND. A.D. 1573. "Agnes Greyll" was appointed "collector for lands called Borrowland" (C. C. R.).

BOULTER'S LOCK. T. M. NO. 1854 ; O. M. NO. 31.

Name derived from bolting, a term used for sifting or dressing wheat flour.

Boulter's Lock signifies the Flour Miller's Lock.

The present lock acquired its name from an old lock at Taplow Mills which was done away with when the present cut and pound lock were made. The old lock was really the Miller's Lock, which admitted vessels from the river into the mill stream.

BOWDEN'S GREEN. O. M. NO. 247. It takes its name from Thomas Bowden, who, A.D. 1609, occupied a house on Cockmarsh Hill and a grove called Cockden Grove, contiguous to this piece of common. At that time Bowden's Green was known as Old House

Green. "Thomas Bowden sells to Reid one little cottage adjoining Old House Green, near Heathfield Gate." *See* Oldhouse Green.

BOZLEYS. A.D. 1609. Was the property of Westcott, now probably a part of Great How Field.

Bos (?), Bosa. The first Bishop of East Anglia (Edm.).

BRADCUTTS, FURTHER MIDDLE. T. M. NO. 106; O. M. NO. 322. Formerly Great Middons.

BRADCUTTS, GREAT. T. M. NO. 105; O. M. NO. 322. Was formerly a part of Great Middons.

BRADCUTTS, HITHER. T. M. NO. 107; O. M. NO. 322. Formerly Great Middons.

BRADCUTTS, LITTLE. T. M. NO. 104; O. M. NO. 322. Was Little Middons, "a pasture near Great Middons."

Bradcutts from *brad*, *E.*, broad, spacious; and *cote*, a mud cottage (Taylor); or it may be that Bradcutts is a corruption of Broadcrofts. *See* Broadcrofts.

BRADCUTTS, LOWER. T. M. NO. 108; O. M. NO. 322. Formerly Great Middons.

BRADELEY. A.D. 1359. "John Brid to amend a fence at Bradeley" (C. C. R.).

BRADELHUTH. A.D. 1394. "A barge at Bradelhuth" (C. C. R.). Bradley hythe or wharf. Probably the river bank at the bottom of what is now Stonehouse Lane, belonging to the manor of Bradley.

BRADLEIGH. A.D. 1362. "Margery Husee held one messuage in Bradleigh." (Inq. p.m.)

BRADLEY. A.D. 1562. "John Cheyney prays to be admitted to Bradley" (C. C. R.).

Brad, *E.*, spacious. Ley, *E.*, from *lege*, a meadow (Edm.).

BRADLEY GREEN. A.D. 1609. Probably some

portion of what is now known as Winter Hill
Common.

BRADWELL. A.D. 1480. In the manor of Cookham
(C. C. R.).

BREWERS, GREAT. T. M. NO. 791 ; O. M. NO. 138.

BREWERS, LITTLE. T. M. NO. 800 ; O. M. NO. 145.
Name of a former owner.

BRIANS. A.D. 1494. " Sir William Danvers elected
collector for Brians " (C. C. R.).

BRIDGE CLOSE. A.D. 1609. " Thomas Austen owned
a Close of Meadow near Maidenhead Bridge called
Bridge Close."

BROADCROFTS. A.D. 1609. Prentall had 1½ acres
arable near Broadcrofts hedge.
Brad, *E.*, spacious ; croft, *E.*, a field or appropriated
ground (Edm.).

BROADCROFTS COPPICE. A.D. 1609. Belonging
to Bradleys.

BROADLEAZE. A.D. 1609. Part of Pinkneys. Now
Long Shot.

BROADMEAD. A.D. 1609. Belonging to Bradleys.
Brad, *E.*, spacious ; med or mæd, a meadow. *See*
Broadmead, Upper.

BROADMEAD. A.D. 1609. Belonging to Babham.
Broadmead and Longmead were afterwards Lady
Mead, from the old oak called " My Lady," then Hill
Mead. Now Fishery Meadow.

BROADMEAD, LOWER. T. M. NO. 36 ; O. M. NO. 7.
Formerly Cockmarsh Mead.

BROADMEAD, UPPER. T. M. NO. 35 ; O. M. NO. 6.
Formerly **Broadmead**, Bradleys.

BROKE, LE. A.D. 1532. " The several waters of
Thomas Annesley called Le Broke " (Maid. Corp.
Records).

3

BROMEHILL. A.D. 1609. An open arable field of 46 acres amongst eight owners. Comprising what is now on the Tithe map Furze Hill, Little Cannon Down, and Rook Hill.

Name doubtless from the broom plant growing there.

BRUSH HILL. *See* Bush Hill Slade.

BUCK CLOSE. T. M. NO. 850 ; O. M. NO. 38.

BUGH ASSILS. A.D. 1609. Belonged to Babham.

BUGHAVILLS. A.D. 1609. Belonged to Cherman ; before him to Babham. Probably Little Slades.

BUGHAZELS. T. M. NO. 761 ; O. M. NO. 308.

Formerly **Bugh-assils.**

Bug, Buck, *E.*, from *boc*, a book or copyhold ; hasel from *haesl*, the hazel tree.

BULLOCKS. T. M. NO. 404 ; O. M. NO. 479 (part of).

BULLOX LEE. A.D. 1609. Part of Bullox Manor. It represented, what on the Tithe map is shown as, Bullocks and Great Whitlea Hare Warren.

BULLOX, MANOR OF. A.D. 1609. The name comes from a former owner or occupier.

A.D. 1225. Richard Bullok paid a fine of one mark for land in Sutton (Roberts excerpt).

A.D. 1423. In the will of John Luffenham mention is made of Richard Bullock's house ; it is the house at the right-hand corner of the Church yard Gate.

A.D. 1445. Richard Bulloke was witness to a grant from John Blakke of a watermill called Reymulles (Bodleian deeds).

The Bulloks or Bullox may have been of the same family as the Bullocks of Bullock's Hatch, in Bray *See* Kerry's Bray.

BULLOX WATER. A.D. 1609. A stream belonging to the manor of Bullox.

BULLS, THE. A.D. 1609. Belonged to Weldon. Is probably now a part of Great Ley Field.

BULLS CLOSE END. A.D. 1609. Belonged to Mattingley.

BURIAL GROUND SHOOTING TO. T. M. NOS. 2132, 2134, 2136; O. M. NOS. 60, 61, 63. A part of Maidenhead Field.

BURNETT'S GREEN. O. M. NO. 219. John Burnett lived in a cottage, now pulled down, abutting on this piece of common.

BURROWS. A.D. 1609. Belonged to Cock.

BURY, LE. A.D. 1515. In the tenure of John Osborne (C. C. R.). Probably Aldebury, *q. v.*

BUSH HILL. A.D. 1609. Belonged to Weldon. *See* Bush Hill Slade.

BUSH HILL SLADE. T. M. NOS. 627, 628; O. M. NO. 416.

BUSHIE PLOTT CLOSE. A.D. 1609. Belongs to Bodley. *See* Bush Hill Slade.

BUTCHER DICK'S MEADOW. T. M. NO. 1805; O. M. NO. 9.

BUTLER'S CLOSE. A.D. 1598. Sir R. Wenman sells to Dorothy Fitzwilliam one meadow called Butler's Close.

BUTLER'S MEAD. A.D. 1609. Belonged to Dorothy Fitzwilliam.

A.D. 1650. John Plummer pays rent for Butler's Mead. (Commonwealth Survey.)

BUTT'S PIECE. T. M. NOS. 1379, 1380; O. M. NO. 635.

BYDELLS. A.D. 1524. Richard Babham appointed Collector for Bydells (C. C. R.).

BYRES, LE. A.D. 1498. John Collingbourne took Le Byres of Lord Sands.

CALVES LEAZE. A.D. 1609. Part of Bullox. *See* Calves Ley and Little Calves Ley.

CALVES LEY. T. M. NO. 470; O. M. NO. 498.

CALVES LEY, LITTLE. T. M. NO. 471; O. M. NO. 498.

CAMLEY CORNER. A.D. 1609. Mentioned in the boundaries of Cookham Parish.

CANNON COPPICE. T. M. NO. 1288; O. M. NO. 378.

CANNON COURT FARM HOMESTEAD. T. M. NO. 1285; O. M. NO. 580. The manor of Cannon, or Connon, formerly belonged to the Abbey of Cirencester.

CANNON DOWN. A.D. 1609. Belonged to Weldon.

CANNON DOWN. T. M. NOS. 1256, 1257; O. M. NO. 567 (part of).

CANNON DOWN, GREAT. T. M. NO. 985; O. M. NOS. 400, 404.

CANNON DOWN, LITTLE. T. M. NO. 1270; O. M. NO. 567.

CANNON EYOTT. A.D. 1636. An eyot in the river Thames (Inq. held at Maidenhead).

CARTER SHED. T. M. NOS. 542, 561; O. M. NO. 410 (part of).

CARTER SHED MEADOW. T. M. NO. 282; O. M. NO. 356.

CARTER'S FARM. A.D. 1650. Mathews paid 13s. rent for Carter's Farm.
A.D. 1650. Brice paid 4d. rent for part of Carter's Farm (Commonwealth Survey).

CARTER'S FIELD. T. M. NO. 1274; O. M. NO. 413 (part of).

CARTER'S SLADE. A.D. 1664. Abigail Hamerton sells John Dodson one acre in Sutton by Carter's Slade (private doc.).

CARTHOUSE CLOSE. Probably Carter's. *See* Drying Ground.

CASTLE HILL. The road out of Maidenhead to Reading. It acquires the name from the Windsor Castle Inn at the top of the hill. *See* Folly Hill.

CAT MOOR. T. M. NO. 1312 ; O. M. NO. 512. Formerly **Catsey Field.**

CATSEY FIELD. A.D. 1609. Belonged to Weldon.
Cat and Eye Island. Probably a swampy piece of ground belonging to Louches. *See* Cat Moor.

CHALK PIT KENTS. T. M. NO. 1488 ; O. M. NO. 767.

CHALK PIT SHOT. T. M. NO. 1690 ; O. M. NOS. 59, 101.

CHECKER FERE. A.D. 1609. Roger Holdernesse holds two acres arable land in Checkerfere within Sutton.
A.D. 1650. Roger Holdernesse pays 8*d.* for rent of Chequer Acre (Commonwealth Survey).
Checker, and fere or fare, *E.*, from *faer*, a way (Edm.).

CHOKE LANE. The road by Louches Farm to Bigfrith Common.

CHURCHFIELD. A.D. 1609. Belonged to Weldon. Was a part of the glebe land belonging to the Abbey of Cirencester. *See* Churchfield, Upper.

CHURCHFIELD, LOWER. T. M. NO. 1303 ; O. M. NO. 413 (part of).

CHURCHFIELD, MIDDLE. T. M. NO. 1302 ; O. M. NO. 413 (part of).

CHURCHFIELD, UPPER. T. M. NO. 1307 ; O. M. NO. 412.

CLARKE'S MEADOW. T. M. NO. 2259 ; O. M. NO. 185.

CLATTAMS. A.D. 1609. Farmer held a close at the Dean called Clattams. Clat, *E.*, from *glat*, a gap. The ancient Clatfordtun is now Claverton (Earle's Philology).

Glat or Clat-ham, the ham or settlement of the Gap or Hollow, probably where the present Dean hamlet is.

COCKDEN GROVE. A.D. 1609. Cockden Grove on Cockmarsh Hill, in the occupation of Thomas Bowden.

Cock, *E.*, little ; den, *E.*, a hollow (Edm.).

COCKMARSH CLOSE, UPPER. T. M. NO. 40 ; O. M. NO. 88.

COCKMARSH COMMON. A.D. 1609. "Unto the inhabitants of Cookham for the whole year." Estimated at 70 acres.

A.D. 1650. Estimated at 120 acres, viz. 92 acres meadow and a steep hill (Commonwealth Survey).

COCKMARSH COMMON. T. M. NO. 175 ; O. M. NOS. 58, 78. Estimated at 134 acres.

There are several ancient tumuli in Cockmarsh. Four of these were opened and examined about the year 1877 by Mr. Alfred H. Cocks, of Great Marlow. The largest one, a mound of some considerable size, proved to be the burial-place, by cremation, of a British female. The second was a Saxon burial. The third contained the burnt remains of a child. In the fourth were found the skull and bones of a small horse, and with them the neck of a seventeenth century bottle.

COCKMARSH HILL. A.D. 1609. Belonged to Woodyour. *See* Cockmarsh Close, Upper.

COCKMARSH HILL. T. M. NO. 38 ; O. M. NO. 89.

COCKMARSH MEAD. A.D. 1609. Belonged to Sharpe. Now a part of Lower Broad Mead.

COCKSFARME. A.D. 1609. Or Luffenhams. At some earlier time this had belonged to Babham.

COKDONSEE. A.D. 1451. "William Norreys held Cokdonsee (Kerry's Bray)."

A.D. 1463. Thomas Babham has a hedge open at Cokdonse (C. C. R.).

A.D. 1527. Thomas Carter does fealty for 3 virgates of land called Cokdonse (C. C. R.).

COKEHAM LANE. A.D. 1527 (C. C. R.).
This was in Maidenhead, near Market Street.

COLLEGE, GREAT. T. M. NO. 727; O. M. NO. 249 (part of).

COLLEGE, LITTLE. T. M. NO. 734; O. M. NO. 358.
This property formerly belonged to Eton College.

COLLINGBOURNE STYLE. A.D. 1463. It is reported that a ditch is obstructed at Collingbourne Style (C. C. R.).
Named probably from some neighbouring owner or occupier. *See* Le Byres.

COMMON DOWN. A.D. 1609. Probably a part of Cannon Down and Rooks Hill.

COMMON FIELDS. A.D. 1609. These belonged largely to Babham.

COMYSLANE. A.D. 1514. "Thomas Cutler is presented for closing Comyslane" (C. C. R.).

CONEY CLOSE. A.D. 1609. It belonged to Sharpe. *See* Coney Close.

CONEY CLOSE. T. M. NO. 55; O. M. NO. 85.

CONEY CLOSE GROVE. A.D. 1609. Belonged to Sharpe. *See* Coney Coppice.

CONEY COPPICE. T. M. NO. 54; O. M. NO. 84.

COOKHAM, or Cocham, as it appears to have been written in the thirteenth century; also Cokham in the fourteenth; Cokeham in the fifteenth; now Cookham.
Note.—There is a Cokeham in Sussex, now a part of the parish of Sompting, which was in the twelfth century a chapelry of the Knights Templars, and was then spelt Cocham. At the end of the sixteenth century it appears to have been spelt Cookham,

whilst the present Ordnance map spelling is Coke-ham.

It has been suggested that as the ham or home field would naturally be near to the ham itself, Cox-borrow, an ancient enclosure adjoining Ham Field, was probably the site of the early Saxon settlement or hamlet.

Cock, *E.*, little ; ham, *E.*, home or village (Edm.).

COOKHAM COURT HOUSE. A.D. 1609. Probably the old court-house at North Town.

Lord Norreys had land in Maidenhead Field near the court-house.

COOKHAM DEAN. The hamlet on the road from Cookham to Bisham in the valley or hollow.

Dene, *E.*, a hollow (Edm.). *See also* Clattams.

COOKHAM DEAN COMMON. O. M. NO. 256.

COOKHAM FIELD. A.D. 1609. Arable, with an area of 36 acres, belonging to Westcott.

COOKHAM GROVE. *See* Grove, The.

COOKHAM MARSH. *See* Marsh Meadow.

COOKHAM MOOR. A.D. 1609. Common of pastur-age to the inhabitants all the year. Estimated area 7 acres.

COOKHAM MOOR. O. M. NO. 354.

COOKHAM POUND. A.D. 1609. Wood had a small house near Cookham Pound.

COOKHAM RAY. *See* Ray Field.

COOKHAM STONE. A.D. 1506. The warrener to hold sports at Cookham Stone (C. C. R.). *See* Tarry Stone.

COOK'S FARM. A.D. 1615. On the south of the Burrow Closes in Cookham. (Will of William Cock.)

A.D. 1759. Cook's or Hamerton's Farmhouse was held by Richard Ovey (private doc.).

COOKSBRED. A.D. 1609.

COPPICE FARM, or KING'S COPPICE FARM.
T. M. NO. 858 ; O. M. NO. 50.
A part of what in the Survey of 1609 was shown as the North and South Coppices.

COPPICES. A.D. 1609. Land belonging to Cutler.

COPYNS. A.D. 1515. Lands called John Copyns, in the tenure of William Est.
A.D. 1523. By order of the Queen Katherine of Arragon, John Copynger, groom of the king's robes, had twelve beech trees from Inwood (C. C. R.).

CORDWALLIS FARM. O. M. NO. 2076.

CORN CLOSE. A.D. 1609. Belonged to Sharpe.

COSTALLO. A.D. 1609. Part of Harwoods.
Gos, *E.*, gorse (Edm.).

COURT HOUSE CLOSE. A.D. 1609. At North Town, belonging to Poole.

COURT HOUSE LANE. Near the Union workhouse.
O. M. NO. 783.

COW PASTURE. T. M. NO. 1201 ; O. M. NO. 678 (part of).

COXBORROW. T. M. NO. 661 ; O. M. NO. 331 (part of).
Borrow or burgh, *E.*, a fortified hill or town (Edm.) ; an earthwork, hence a town (Taylor).

CRANEFIELD, GREAT. T. M. NO. 980 ; O. M. NO. 398 (part of).

CREKE, THE. A.D. 1636. Between Gladman's Eiott and New Eiott. (Inq. held at Maidenhead.)

CROOKED CLOSE. T. M. NO. 56 ; O. M. NO. 87.

CROSS SHOT. T. M. NOS. 1150—1157 ; O. M. NO. 667.
Part of Southey Field.

CRUTCHFIELD CORNER. T. M. NOS. 1387, 1555 ;
O. M. NO. 139. Part of Maidenhead Field.
A.D. 1392. Thomas Cruchefelde was a joint owner of Ray Mills (Bodleian documents).

CRUTCHFIELD CORNER SHOT. T. M. NO. 1554; O. M. NOS. 142, 143 (part of). Part of Maidenhead Field.

CULHAM'S CLOSE. T. M. NOS. 2286, 2287; O. M. NO. 193.

CULVER CLOSE. A.D. 1609. Belonged to Pinkneys. Culver, calver, *B.*, from *coll fa*, the place of the hazel (Edm.).

CURBY CLOSE, or SPRING CLOSE. T. M. NO. 1736; O. M. NO. 611.
Car, care, a pool ; by, *D.*, an abode (Edm.).

CURTEYS LANE. A.D. 1506. Tithing man of Great Bradley presents that the Prior of Bustleham do make a new gate at Curteys Lane (C. C. R.).
Curteys Lane, or Courthouse Lane ; probably either Stonehouse Lane, or the lane leading to Bowden's Green.

DABSTONE LANE. T. M. NOS. 2140—2144 ; O. M. NOS. 109, 110.

DABSTONE SHOT. T. M. NO. 2107 ; O. M. NO. 67 (part of). Part of Maidenhead Field.
Is Dab a corruption of Dag, a Saxon personal name ? Dægston ?

DANE CLOSE. A.D. 1609. Part of Pinkneys. Probably now a part of Beeching Grove.
Dane, down, *E.*, from *dune*, a grassy hillock (Edm.).

DANEFIELD. A.D. 1609. Belonged to Sharpe. Probably Tuleys is now a part of it.

DANEFIELD GROVE. A.D. 1609. Belonged to Sharpe. Possibly Upper Short Crops forms a part of this.

DARLINGS. T. M. NO. 1458 ; O. M. NO. 717.
Darlin, *B.*, from *dar*, oak, and *llain*, a patch (Edm.).

DEAN CLOSE. A.D. 1609. Belonged to Nokes. Probably Little Terrys.

DEAN CLOSE. T. M. NO. 82 ; O. M. NO. 121.

DEAN CLOSE. T. M. NO. 95 ; O. M. NO. 161.

DEAN FARM, or LOWER WINTER HILL FARM. T. M. NO. 74 ; O. M. NO. 118.

DEANE FARM. T. M. NO. 85 ; O. M. NO. 124.

DEAN STILE. A.D. 1672. With the coppice a part of the manor of Cannons.

DEANE HOUSE. A.D. 1609. Belonged to Nokes. Dean Farm (?).

DEANFIELD. A.D. 1609. Arable, of 45 acres, amongst nine owners. *See* Deanfields.

DEANFIELD. T. M. NO. 1507 ; O. M. NO. 770.

DEANFIELD CLOSE. A.D. 1609. Belonged to Weldon. Now a part of Upper and Lower Deanfields.

DEANFIELD SHAW. T. M. NO. 1281; O. M. NO. 588.

DEANFIELDS. T. M. NO. 1507; O. M. NO. 770 (part of)·

DEANFIELDS, LOWER. T. M. NO. 1297 ; O. M. NO. 590.

DEANFIELDS, UPPER. T. M. NO. 1280 ; O. M. NO. 590.

DEDEMAN'S LANE. A.D. 1456. Reported—branches are cut from the trees at Dedemanslane (C. C. R.).

DEVENYSHE HOUSE. A.D. 1359. An ancient house in Maidenhead (Gorham). Probably from a family of that name.

DIAL CLOSE. T. M. NO. 67 ; O. M. NO. 94 (part of).
  There was a very large barn standing on Dial Close, more like a monastic grange barn than one on an ordinary farm homestead. This was pulled down

some time between the years 1830 and 1840. There was also a dipping well in the Close, approached by a flight of old steps; it was nearly concealed by a dense undergrowth. *See* Dyall Close.

The house newly built on this ground is named Irlas. *See* Irlas.

DICKERLEAZE CLOSE. A.D. 1609. Belonged to Turner.

A.D. 1574. Thomas Use by will leaves sundry acres of rye on the east side of Dyckerleas.

Dike or Dyke, *E.*, an entrenchment (Edm.). *See* Dickerleys Meadow.

DICKERLEAZE HILL CLOSE. A.D. 1609. Belonged to Turner. *See* Dickerleys and the Lakes.

DICKERLEYS AND THE LAKES. T. M. NO. 993; O. M. NO. 415. Formerly **Dickerleaze Hill Close.**

DICKERLEYS HILL AND SHEARLINGS. T. M. NO. 1207; O. M. NO. 663 (part of).

DICKERLEYS MEADOW. T. M. NO. 1205; O. M. NO. 663 (part of).

DISMALS LONG. T. M. NO. 1366; O. M. NO. 540 (part of).

DISMALS LONG ROADWAY. T. M. NO. 1358; O. M. NO. — Pathway between the gardens of Ditton House and Pinkneys Farm homestead. *See* **Disners.**

DISMARKS. A.D. 1502. John Grove does fealty for lands at Dismarks (C. C. R.).

DISNERS. A.D. 1609. Smith owned Disners.

Dy, *B.*, a house (Edm.).

The lands called Pinkneys and Disners, or Dismals, adjoin each other. In the Hurley Charters, published by the Rev. F. T. Wethered, in a quit claim by Robert de Lullebrook to the Prior and Convent of Hurley, dated Sept. A.D. 1322, two of the witnesses are Henry Pynkeney and John Disners.

DISNERS COPPICE. A.D. 1609. Smith owned Disners Coppice. Probably T. M. NO. 1363 ; O. M. NO. 559.

DISNERS CROFT. A.D. 1609. Smith owned Disners Croft. Probably T. M. NO. 1364 ; O. M. NO. 560.

DISNERS PASTURE. A.D. 1609. Bodley owned Disners Pasture. Probably T. M. 1357 ; O. M. NO. 542.

DITTON HOUSE. T. M. NO. 1355 ; O. M. NO. 546.
A.D. 1505. By her will Alice Bukland, of Maydenhith, left to Henry Annesley a cottage called Benett, of Dytton, in the parish of Cookham.
Dit, *E.*, place enclosed by an entrenchment or ditch (Edm.).

DODSONS. T. M. NO. 331 ; O. M. — Appears as Rosebank. Named after Sir John Dodson, who built the house. He was high sheriff of Berks, A.D. 1716. His monument is on the south wall of Cookham Church.

DODSONS CLOSE. T. M. NOS. 237, 238 ; O. M. NO. 419.

DOLLYS FARM. T. M. NO. 1795 ; O. M. NO. 655.
Dol, *B.*, a bend of a stream (Edm.).

DOLLYS HILL. T. M. NO. 1924; O. M. NO. 24 (part of).

DOOVERS. A.D. 1609. A part of Bradleys. Probably Doovers Wood, now annexed to Bisham parish.
Dover, *B.*, from *dwfwr*, water (Edm.).

DOULES, THE. A.D. 1696. " Howland pays 9*s.* 6*d.* land tax for the Doules."

DOVEHOUSE CLOSE. A.D. 1609. Part of Bullox. *See* Pigeon House Close.

DRAKES CLOSE. T. M. NO. 2056 ; O. M. NO. 111 (part of). Now Elendene and the Firs. *See* Hardegrepys.

DRY CLOSE. *See* Gravelly Close.

DRY WELLS. T. M. NO. 1199; O. M. NO. 478 (part of).

DRYING GROUND. T. M. NO. 286; O. M. NO. 436 (part of).

DYALL CLOSE. A.D. 1609. A part of Bradleys. The "old house," probably a Saxon homestead, stood where Winter Hill Farm homestead now stands, *i. e.* between Dyall Close (the old house close) on the west and Old House Green (now Bowden's Green) on the east. *See* Dial Close.

Dy, *B.*, a house ; al, *E.*, from *eald*, old (Edm.).

Note.—The name Dial Close has been appropriated for a residence on what was known as Farm Coppice at the west side of Winter Hill, and the house now built on Dial Close has been named Irlas. Edmunds gives ir, *E.*, as a cognate word with ar, *B.*, meaning land ; and las, *B.*, an old word meaning a stream. So that Irlas (a recent name) would indicate the river land or river property.

DYARS. A.D. 1609. Belonged to Hobby.

EASTMOOR HILL MEADOW. T. M. NO. 2282; O. M. NO. 219.

EASTMORE HILLS. A.D. 1609. Part of Pinkneys.

A.D. 1650. Mrs. Sanders pays 6s. 2d. rent for Hakes and Eastmore Hills (Commonwealth Survey).

A.D. 1683. Meadow in Eastmore Hills given by George Townsend. *See* Eastmoor Hill Meadow.

ELDERSTUBB. A.D. 1609. Part of Pinkneys. Probably a part of what is now Oaken Grove.

ELDFIELD. A.D. 1609. A part of Ham Field. *See also* Alvill.

ELDFIELD HATCH. A.D. 1609. Probably the entrance to Ham Field, just above Nightingale Place. *See* Alville Hatche.

ELDFIELD HILL. A.D. 1609.

ELLINGTON, or KNIGHT ELLINGTON. A.D.
1189. Simon de Pinkeni as to land at Helington.

A.D. 1198. William de l'Hoo gave Jordan the Forester six marks in silver for one virgate of land and appurtenances at Elinton. (Hunter Fines Roberts excerpt.)

The Abbot of Cirencester grants to Lord William of Polesworth permission to hold an oratory in his court of Elinton. (Cirencester Cartulary.)

A.D. 1391. William Elynton, of Cokham, grants land, &c., to John Pynkeny.

Elynden family: John Elynden, A.D. 1333; Henry Elyngton, A.D. 1358; Johñs. Elinton, A.D. 1454 (Kerry's Bray).

The name Ellington comes from Ey, or Ea-ing-ton. Ey, E., island ; ing, E., meadow ; tun, E., town. The island meadow settlement exactly describes a piece of pasturage ground near Spencers Farm homestead, now known as North Moor, q. v. It may also be well to say that Taylor, in his 'Words and Places,' mentions the Ellings as one of the Norse families which invaded and settled in Britain.

Knight Ellington. Is not this first name acquired from the Knights Templars? They had other property in Cookham (for instance, Hemmings). Upon the dissolution of the Order of Knights Templars, Bisham seems *not* to have passed, with the greater part of their estates, to the Knights of St. John, it having been granted in fee to Hugh le Spencer, jun. (Dugdale and Tanner's Not.)

A.D. 1325. There was an inquiry as to certain messuages in Cocham granted to John le Spencer, & vt. Aldebury. (Inq. post damn., 13 Ed. 2nd.) Aldebury is a part of the manor of Spencers and Knight Ellington. *See* Aldebury ; also Spencers.

Is John incorrectly written for Hugh le Spencer?

ELLINGTON, SOUTH. *See* Maidenhead.

ELMS, THE. T. M. NOS. 320, 327, 328, 337, 339; O. M. The Elms, Cookham. The Elms was formerly part of the manor of Lollybrook.

EMORGES. A.D. 1609. Belonged to Mattingley.

ENGLIS HEYES. A.D. 1523. A croft called Englis Heyes (C. C. R.).

EYROME. A.D. 1609. "Sometime in the tenure of John Babham" (Minist. Acts).

FAG END. O. M. NO. 37. A.D. 1322. As to rents. The lands of Fag "Nothing," because it remains yet on the lord's hands, being barren. (Exch. Accts., 15 & 16 Ed. 2nd.)

Fag, an abbreviation of Faga, a Saxon proper name. Readers of 'Ivanhoe' may remember that Sir Walter Scott gives to Gurth's (the swineherd) dog the name of Fag.

Fag End, at the west end of Cookham parish, perpetuates the name of an old Saxon family, as does Babham End, at the east end of the parish.

FAGERS. A.D. 1650. John Hamerton pays 5s. 9d. for Fagers (Commonwealth Survey).

FARM COPPICE. A.D. 1609. Part of Harwoods. *See* Fern Close.

FARM COPPICE. T. M. NO. 829; O. M. NO. 12. (Now called Dial Close.)

FARTHINGS. A.D. 1609. Belonged to Page.

A.D. 1369. William Wymere acquires lands which were of Thomas Ferthing in Cokham (C. C. R.).

A.D. 1390. Thomas White bequeaths to John Lawrence of Bray his lands called Ferthings (C. C. R.).

A.D. 1524. Robert Fowler held land called Fferdings (C. C. R.).

A.D. 1576. Thomas Hill leaves to John Roberts by will his lands Lawrence and Farthings, otherwise Yanze (C. C. R.).

A.D. 1650. John Roberts pays 10s. 2d. rent for Farthings (Commonwealth Survey).

FEENS MOOR. A.D. 1609. Newbery held land at Feens Moor.

FEENS MOOR. T. M. NO. 1804 ; O. M. NO. 7.

FEENS SHAW. T. M. NO. 719 ; O. M. NO. 361 (part of).

FERN CLOSE. T. M. NO. 970; O. M. NO. 257 (part of).

FFABERS. A.D. 1522. "A collector was elected for land called Ffabers" (C. C. R.).

FFINPOLE. A.D. 1517. "Sheep put to pasture in Ffinpole" (C. C. R.).

FFULPOLE MEDE. A.D. 1457. "A meadow called Ffulpole Mede" (C. C. R.).

FFULTON MEYDE. A.D. 1489. "An enclosure called Ffulton Meyde" (C. C. R.).

FFYNES MORE. A.D. 1488. "A ditch not cleaned out at Ffynes More" (C. C. R.).

FILBYS. T. M. NO. 750; O. M. NO. 310 (part of).
Fil, *E., feld*, a field, by, *D.,* an abode (Edm.).

FISHERY MEADOW. T. M. NO. 402 ; O. M. NOS. 480 and 481. Formerly The Hill. *See* Broadmead.

FOLLY FIELD. T. M. NO. 1521 ; O. M. NO. 201.
Folly, *E.,* from *folc ley*, the people's land held in common (Edm.).

FOLLY HILL. *See* Castle Hill, for which the name has been changed in quite recent years.

In his 'History of Newberry,' Mr. Walter Money notes, "There are certain words which are constantly observed along the lines of Roman ways, and among them is Folly."

About the year 1885, when digging foundations for the house on Castle Hill known as "Verona," on the Bray side of the roadway, the unearthing of some pieces of tile and pottery led to the discovery, under

5

the superintendence of Mr. Rutland, of the remains of a Roman house, which must have been one of considerable size and importance. This not only goes to confirm the correctness of Mr. Money's observation, but also shows that the old name of "Folly Hill," which had been retained for so many centuries, was not without its significance.

FOLLY SHOT. T. M. NOS. between 1583 and 1627 ; O. M. NO. 145. Part of Maidenhead Field.

FORLEAZE ACRE. A.D. 1650. John Roberts paid 6d. rent on Forleaze Acre (Commonwealth Survey).

FORMOSA PLACE. T. M. NO. 380 ; O. M. NO. 462.
This house was built by Admiral Sir George Young (see his monument on the east end of the south aisle in Cookham Church), and, independently of the beauty of its situation, Formosa probably owes its name to Cape Formosa and the island of Formosa ; off both of these places Sir George Young had been stationed.

FOTTERS. A.D. 1532. A tenement in Maidenhead belonging to Thomas Annesley (Corporation Records).

FOUKETTS. A.D. 1500. John Barton, of Burnehm, co. Bucks, leaves "My tenement called Fouketts to Cokeh'm Church." Will of John Barton (Berks Arch. Journal, April, 1894).

FOUNTAIN MEAD. A.D. 1609. A common meadow, in area about 32 acres, amongst twelve owners.
Fountain Mead was, I think, in earlier times, either Full Pool or Fulton Mead. Either name would be fitting, and both of them significant. At its north-west corner was a swampy marsh, the deepest part of which was probably always full of muddy water. Ful, Fullan, E., foul or dirty. Or again Ful, a corruption of fowl, and ton, settlement, would signify a wild fowl resort or breeding place, for which it would have been specially suited. It is now known as Poulton Mead.

FULLPOOL MEAD. A.D. 1609. A part of Fountain Mead.

A.D. 1505. By her will Alice Bukland bequeaths land in Fullpole Mede.

FULTON MEAD. *See* also Ffulton Mead.

A.D. 1561. Thos. Weldon held eleven acres in Fowlton Mead (Survey, 3rd Eliz.).

FURZE HILL. T. M. NOS. 692, 693, 694; O. M. NOS. 363 and 365 (part of).

FURZE PIECE. T. M. NO. 50; O. M. NO. 88 (part of).

FURZE PLATT. T. M. NO. 1377; O. M. NOS. 606 and 607.

FYNESMORE. A.D. 1523. "A ditch obstructed at Fynesmore" (C. C. R.).

GARRETTS. A.D. 1609. Belonged to Cordell.

GASCATE. A.D. 1609. Durdent had land in Langdon called Gascate.

Gars, *E.*, from *gers*, grass, and Gates, *E.*, from *gaet*, a goat (Edm.).

GAYHOLE FURLONG. T. M. NOS. between 477 and 498; O. M. NO. 411. A part of Sutton Field.

Gay as a suffix, *N. F.*, a form of *haie*, an enclosure. Gay as a prefix, *E.*, from *gaed*, a goad, also a man's name (Edm.).

GELDINGS. T. M. NO. 57; O. M. NO. 99.

GELDON'S CLOSE. A.D. 1609. Belonged to Hare. *See* Geldings.

GENTLE CLOSE. A.D. 1609. Was a part of Lawrence's, probably now a part of John's Close.

GIBRALTAR CLOSE. T. M. NO. 16; O. M. NO. 62.

GIBRALTAR WOOD. T. M. NO. 14; O. M. NO. 61.

GILDON'S GROVE. A.D. 1650. Sir Edward Mansfield pays 2s. 2d. for Gildon's Grove (Commonwealth Survey).

GILES. A.D. 1609. Belonged to Harris. *See* Giles.

GILES. T. M. NO. 1499 ; O. M. NO. 777 (part of).

GINGER HILL. A.D. 1609. Davie had land there ; it was a part of Maidenhead Field near to Wellhouse Field.

GLADMAN'S EYOTT. An island in the river Thames.

GLEDINGORE. A.D. 1511. A meadow called Gledingore (C. C. R.).

GODFREYS, GREAT. T. M. NO. 904 ; O. M. NO. 208.

GODFREYS, LITTLE. T. M. NO. 885 ; O. M. NO. 208.
After a family so named, who were Woodwards to the Manor, and as such occupied this property. Its earlier name was the Woodwards.

GOD'S CLOSE. T. M. NO. 1793 ; O. M. NO. 651.

GOOSE MEADOW. T. M. NOS. 378 and 391 ; O. M. NOS. 455 and 463. It is a part of Odney.

GRANGE, THE. A.D. 1482. " A path leading from Maidenhead to the Grange " (C. C. R.).

GRASSEHILL. A.D. 1672. A meadow, part of the Manor of Cannons.

GRAVELLY CLOSE, or DRY CLOSE. T. M. NOS. 721 and 722 ; O. M. NOS. 361 and 382. Was formerly **Stoney Croft.**

GRAVELLY CLOSE, LOWER. T. M. NO. 696 ; O. M. NO. 363.

GRAVELLY CLOSE, UNDER. T. M. NOS. 691 and 695 ; O. M. NO. 363.

GRAVEL PIT CLOSE. A.D. 1609. Part of Saracen's Head property, probably part of Gravel Pit Close.

GRAVEL PIT CLOSE. T. M. NO. 1268 ; O. M. NO. 58.

GREAT CRANES. A.D. 1609. Part of Harwoods. It may have acquired its name from an occupant, as

A.D. 1608, one Hugh Crane was joint tenant in Ray Mills. *See* Cranefield, Great.

GREAT FIELD. T. M. NO. 1275 ; O. M. NO. 565.

GREAT GROVE. A.D. 1609. Belonged to Hunter. It was, I think, a part of Odney.

GREAT GROVE. A.D. 1609. A part of Woodmancutts. *See* Great College.

GREAT LEYS. *See* Leys, Great and Little.

GREAT MIDDONS. A.D. 1609. A part of Bradleys. *See* **Bradcutts.**

GREAT ORCHARD, LOUCHES. T. M. NO. 1311 ; O. M. NO. 269.

GREENHILL LAKE. T. M. NO. 1204 ; O. M. NO. 665.

GREEN LANE FURLONG. T. M. NO. 445 ; O. M. NO. 490 (part of).

GREEN LANE PIGHTLE. T. M. NO. 448 ; O. M. NO. 491. Part of Sutton Field.

GREEN, LAY'S. *See* Ley's Green.

GREENWAYS LAKE CLOSE. A.D. 1609. Belonged to Turner. *See* Greenhill Lake.

GROVE, LITTLE. A.D. 1609. It belonged to Hunter. It was, I think, a part of Odney.

GROVE, THE, or COOKHAM GROVE. T. M. NO. 336 ; O. M. NO. 420. Is the name obtained from the Great and Little Grove, which, A.D. 1609, belonged to Jasper Hunter, and were, I think, a part of Odney?

GUIGATE. A.D. 1609. Babham held a fishery in the Thames beginning at the Guigate.

GYRONS LANE. A.D. 1488. A hedge ruinous at Gyrons Lane (C. C. R.).

HAINSWICK. A.D. 1609. Smith had land at Hainswick.

A.D. 1502. John Grove, sen., does fealty for lands called Henyswyke and Dismarks (C. C. R.).

A.D. 1512. Plea of unlawful seizure by John Grove at Haynswyks and Dismarks (C. C. R.).

HAKES. A.D. 1650. Mrs. Sanders pays 1s. 6d. for Eastmorehills and land called Hakes (Commonwealth Survey).

HAKKER'S LAND. A.D. 1514. Re-leased to the Provost of Eton (C. C. R.).

HALLDORE. A.D. 1609. A common arable field, being part of Ham Field. It included 19½ acres amongst seven owners. The name is acquired, I think, from aurus, a draught ox, and dortor or dortarium, a sleeping place (Martin). The field known as the " Six Acres Maidenhead Lane," T. M. NO. 715, which adjoined it, was an old enclosure fenced with a hedge on the north-west and south, and divided from Halldore on the east by a *wide* and steep mere balk, on which a number of blackthorn stubs and bushes evidenced the existence of a hedge at some former period. The steepness of the mere balk indicated that the land on the east had been lowered from it by centuries of ploughing—itself remaining unploughed. This was probably the field where the working oxen of the hamlet were turned out at night to pasture (Prothero, ' Pioneers of Farming ; ' Seebohm, ' Village Communities '), and it is the more probable as the name of an old enclosure on the opposite side of Maidenhead Lane is called Plaistows (*See* Plaistows). Halldoor being that part of Ham Field abreast of the old enclosure would from it acquire a distinguishing name ; just as in other arable fields in which portions of them have distinct names in connection with enclosures abutting on them. *See* Hall Dore.

HALL DORE. T. M. NOS. between 662 and 714 ; O. M. NOS. 324 (part of), 329, 331 (part of).

It included 17½ acres of arable land amongst nine owners. *See* **Halldore.**

HALL DORE SHOT. T. M. NO. 663 ; O. M. NO. 365.

HAM FIELD. A.D. 1609. It was an arable common field of 37 acres amongst eleven owners. Ham, *E.*, a home or village, shows this to have been the field near the settlement.

HAM FIELD. T. M. NOS. between 654 and 710 ; O. M. NOS. 300 to 321. An arable field containing 104 acres amongst thirteen owners. It probably includes Eldfield and other lands that formerly were distinct from Ham Field. That there was a settlement here in very early times is evidenced by the flint implements, especially very fine spear heads, that have been found on this ground.

HAMERTON'S ELMS. T. M. NO. 717 ; O. M. NO. 327. The hedge-rows on the west, north, and east sides of the lower nine acres at Starlings were formerly studded with elm trees (a few of these are still in existence at the bottom of Starling's road), the descendants of trees probably planted by William Hamerton, who was tenant of the land under Sir Thomas Hoby, A.D. 1609. The hedge on the north side then extended some twenty yards further to the east, turning short round to the south-west. When in the year 1845 the roadway from the top of Maidenhead Lane was straightened by carrying it through the nine-acre field, all the elm trees, save the few now remaining, were cut down. The western hedge of the nine acres, with the elm trees, had been cut and grubbed in the year 1841.

HAMERTON'S ELMS FURLONG. T. M. NO 697-9 ; O. M. NOS. 363, 365, 366. A portion of Ham Field abutting on Hamerton's Elms ; hence the name.

HANBEDD. A.D. 1609. A place near Salisbury Pitt called Hanbedd (Exch. Ct. Enquiry).

HANSES WATER. A.D. 1700. Near the head pile of Cookham Ferry.

HARDEGREPYS. A.D. 1488. A tenement of Roger Norreys' called Hardegrepys (C. C. R.).

A.D. 1515. Land and meadow at North Town in the tenure of Robert Drake, called Hardegrepys (C. C. R.). *See* Drake's Close.

HARDING'S CLOSE. T. M. NO. 746 ; O. M. NO. 299. Named probably from some former owner or occupier. A Harding printed and published the account of the deaths by lightning at Eldfield Hatch.

HARDING'S GREEN. O. M. NO. 303. It adjoins Harding's Close, and its name is probably similarly acquired.

HARE WARREN FURLONG. T. M. NOS. between 417 and 472 ; O. M. NO. 472. Part of Sutton field.

HARPAIRE. A.D. 1609. Part of Pound Field, belonging to Bullox.

HARROW LANE. It runs by the side of O. M. NO. 1919 ; and connects the Cookham road with the Marlow road from Maidenhead. It was formerly Wellhouse Field Lane.

HARROW MEADOW. T. M. NO. 1789 ; O. M. NO. 19. Named from the Harrow public house to which it is opposite.

HARTWELLS. T. M. NO. 1295 ; O. M. NO. 516. Probably from a former owner of this name.

A.D. 1570. One Richard Hartwell occupied Tryndle Acre (Gorham).

HARWOODS. A.D. 1609. An old manor belonging to Sir John Herbert. There was the Manor House with six acres of land (*see* Place Orchard) and fifty-two acres of warren ; and also Harwood Mansion House. *See* Mount Farm.

Sir John Herbert was a Privy Councillor and, at or not long before his death, Secretary of State to King James I. He had extensive landed estates in Glamorganshire. His will, in which he is described

as of Cardiff was proved by his widow, Lady
Margaret Herbert, and his son-in-law, Sir William
Dodington, on the 12th December, A.D. 1617. Two
other executors, named Francis Morrice and John
Rogers, renounced probate.

Lady Margaret Herbert probably lived, after his
death, altogether at Harwoods. By her will she
desires to be buried without any manner of pomp,
and she leaves £8 to be distributed amongst the
poorest of Cookham. Sir William Dodington is her
sole executor, and one of the witnesses to her signa-
ture is George Garrard. In the Cookham burial
register (Steele's copy) is the burial of Ladie Margaret
Hurbert 3rd March, A.D. 1625.

Har, *E.*, grey or hoary. Wood, *E.*, from *wuda*, a
wood. Probably the last remaining portion of the
old primeval forest.

HAYCROFTS. A.D. 1696. Thomas Rance paid 1s. 6d.
aid for Haycrofts.

HAYNESWYKE. A.D. 1512. A field called Hayn
wyke (C. C. R.). Probably **Hainswick.**

HEADINGTON COPPICE. T. M. NO. 972 ; O. M. NO
257 (part of). After a former occupier probably.

HEATHFIELD. A.D. 1609. A common arable field
of 47 acres amongst eight owners. *See* Heathfield.

HEATHFIELD CLOSE. A.D. 1609. A part of
Bradley. *See* Heathfield.

HEATHFIELD GATE. A.D. 1609. "Mansion near
to Heathfield Gate."

HEATHFIELD, FURTHER. T. M. NO. 48 ; O. M. NO.
100.

HEATHFIELD, HITHER. T. M. NO. 49 ; O. M. NO.
100.

HEATHFIELDS. A.D. 1609. Belonged to Westcott, is probably now a part of Great How Field.

Heath, *E.*, from *haeth*, a heath (Edm.).

HECHENDEN. A.D. 1547. Cottage and orchard known as Hechenden (C. C. R.).

HECKFORD. A.D. 1553. William Cutler bequeaths a cote known as Hechford (Cook. Wills).

HEMMINGS. A.D. 1609. Late belonging to Lord Sands.

Heming, name of the leader of the Danish Fleet, A.D. 1007 (Edm.).

HEMMINGS. T. M. NOS. 1484–7 ; O. M. NO. 757. Owner Nathaniel Micklem.

Hemmings, Randalls, and Stranges adjoin each other.

HEMYNGS. A.D. 1609. Land near Bigfrith belonging to Francis Micklem.

A.D. 1284. The jurors present that one Heming de Biggefrith was a tenant of the Lord King John, grandfather of the King that now is, of ancient demesne of the Crown, and a certain Elias de Bremble then bailiff of Cokeham alienated the aforesaid tenement, suit and customs into the hands of the Templars of Bustleham (Pleas. quo. warrant, 12 Ed. 1st). *See* Hemmings.

HENDONS. A.D. 1609. Belonged to Bodley. It was a part of the Manor of Heyndens, or Hyndens in Bray (Kerry's Bray).

A.D. 1447. Sir John Norres held (with the Manors of Spencers and Elyngton) the Manor of Heyndons in Cokeham. Sir John's wife was Margaret, Duchess of Norfolk (Kerry's Bray). The Duchess was widow of Shakespeare's " Jockey of Norfolk."

A.D. 1321. William of Hynedone held of Richard Chilton, or Charlton, Abbot of Cirencester, a messuage with a virgate of land in Cokham. This no doubt was what is now Cannon Court.

Farm of Hendons called Redishes farm in Cokeham. *See* Hindhay.

HENDRICKS. T. M. NO. 1508; O. M. NO. 769 (part of).

HENYSWYKE. *See* Hainswick.

HIGHWAY FARM HOMESTEAD. T. M. NO. 1494; O. M. NO. 772.

HILFIELD. A.D. 1609. Belonged to Weldon. *See* Hill Field, Middle, and Lower Church Fields.

HILL, THE. A.D. 1609. Part of Babhams. *See* Fishery Meadow.

HILL CLOSE. A.D. 1609. Belongs to Osborne. *See* Hill Close.

HILL CLOSE. T. M. NO. 96; O. M. NO. 161.

HILL FIELD. T. M. NO. 1301; O. M. NO. 412.

HILL GROVE. T. M. NO. 1341; O. M. NO. 540.

HILL GROVE. A.D. 1609. Belonged to Bradleys. *See* Hill Grove Wood.

HILL GROVE WOOD. T. M. NO. 93; O. M. NO. 160.

HILL PIECE. T. M. NO. 1342; O. M. NO. 539.

HILL PIECE. T. M. NO. 725; O. M. NO. 379.

HILL PIECE SHAW. T. M. NO. 726; O. M. NO. 379.

HINDHAY or LANGTONS. O. M. NO. 532. Part of Hendons.

Hindhay, probably *heah*, *E.*, high; and hay, *E.*, *haga*, enclosed land (Edm.). *See* **Hendons.**

HINDONS. A.D. 1445. Edward Norreys his manor or farm of Redishes or Hindons (Deeds, Bodleian Library). *See* **Hendons.**

HITCHENDON. A.D. 1649. John Geary assigns to John Dodson his mansion in Cokeham called Hitchendon (Private Doc.).

HO, LE HO, HOO, also **HOWE.** One of the tithing divisions.

A.D. 1356. Thomas le Stoke sues Margery le Hert for trespass at Cokham at a place called Le Hoo.

A.D. 1485. View of Frank pledge held at Cokham. John Joly tithing man of Howe presents, &c., &c.

A.D. 1495. Will. Norreys, knight, pays 5s. 7d. relief for three virgates of land at Le Ho. At the same court Roger Morecock tithing man of " Hoo " presents, &c.

A.D. 1523. Roger Osbourne tithing man of Hoo.

A.D. 1524. Richard Turner, constable of Maidenhead and Hoo.

A.D. 1526. Christopher Martin held of the Lady Katherine a certain tenement and lands called Hoo (C. C. R.).

There is no mention of courts being held at La Hoo as at La Legh ; but Court house Lane by Howe Field would indicate the existence, at some former time, of a court house, or a place for holding courts.

Ho, Hoo, Howe, *D.*, a hill (Edm.). *See* Howe Field.

HOCKETT or **ROCHETT.** A.D. 1609. Common of pasturage ; area 20 acres.

The high ground on the west of and adjoining Bigfrith ; it is mostly in Bisham parish. Hoch, *E.*, *heah*, high (Edm.) ; *ette* or *atte*, a place. The cultivated portion is know now as Highwood.

HOGGELDER. A.D. 1609. Belonged to Harris, is now a part of Giles.

HOG CLOSE. T. M. NO. 1191 ; O. M. NO. 685 (part of).

HOG TROUGH. T. M. NO. 865 ; O. M. NO. 204.

Recent name from its supposed (slight) resemblance in shape to this feeding vessel.

HOLLYBUSH, THE. A.D. 1609. Belonged to Smith.

HOLLYBUSH CLOSE. T. M. NO. 42 ; O. M. NO. 89.

In the south-west part of this field are foundations of a dwelling-house or houses.

HOLLYBUSH CLOSE. T. M. NO. 111 ; O. M. NO. 322 (part of).

A holly tree grew in the corner of both these enclosures.

HOLMAN LEAZE. A.D. 1609. Seven acres amongst three owners.

A.D. 1488. " Alice Bukland a ditch in Holmeleys not scoured." *See* Omman Leaze.

Holm, *N.*, a grassy hill by the water, or an island. Leaze, *E.*, a pasture (Edm.). *See* Holman Leaze.

HOLMAN LEAZE. T. M. NOS. 2024—7 ; O. M. NOS. 129, 134.

HOME CLOSE. T. M. NO. 577 ; O. M. NO. 347.

HOME CLOSE. T. M. NO. 768 ; O. M. NO. 157.

HOME CLOSE. T. M. NO. 1289 ; O. M. NO. 578.

HOME CLOSE. T. M. NO. 729 ; O. M. NO. 360.

HOME CLOSE. T. M. NO. 2162 ; O. M. Kidwell's Park (part of).

HOME CLOSE. T. M. NO. 2164 ; O. M. Kidwell's Park (part of).

HOME CLOSE, LITTLE. T. M. NO. 729 ; O. M. NO. 360.

HOME FIELD. A.D. 1609. Belonged to Bodley.

HOME FIELD. A.D. 1609. Part of Harwoods. *See* Great Crains, Louches.

HOME FIELD. A.D. 1609. Parcel of Pinkneys. Part of Beeching Grove, Pinkneys.

HOME FIELD. A.D. 1609. Parcel of Weldon. Part of Great Field, Cannon Court.

HOME FIELD. T. M. NO. 97 ; O. M. NO. 161 (part of).

HOME FIELD. T. M. NO. 1172 ; O. M. NO. 663.

HOME FIELD, HITHER. T. M. NO. 980 ; O. M. NO. 395.

HOME FIELD, LOWER. T. M. NO. 1290 : O. M. NO. 395.

HOME FIELD, UPPER. T. M. NO. 1291 ; O. M. NO. 395.

HOME LEYS. A.D. 1412. Ditch not scoured at Home Leys (C. C. R.).

HOPKINS FIELD. T. M. NO. 1471 ; O. M. NO. 762.

HORSE LEAZE. A.D. 1609. Belonged to Weldon.

HORSTREET. A.D. 1609. Is now represented by the footpath from Wellhouse field to the railway arch at Crawford College. The position of Horstreet is verified by the will of Thomas Osbourne A.D. 1583. He bequeaths an enclosure in North Town Field bounding on the weste ende upon Horstreet, and the north side upon Wellhouse feelde Lane (this is now the Harrow Lane), and on the east the Lord Bakers, and on the south Mr. W. Weldon. The field thus bequeathed is the old enclosure T. M. NOS. 1786 and 1787 ; O. M. NO. 34. *See also* **Hurstreet.**

HORTON GRANGE. T. M. NO. 1876 ; O. M. NO. 30.

So called by Mr. Henry Seebohm, who built the house in the year 1891 to perpetuate the name of a property near Bradford in Yorkshire, belonging to his family who formerly resided there. *See* Sandhill Close.

HOWARD'S CLOSE also **ATTE HOWE.** A.D. 1609. Belonged to Roberts.

HOWFIELD, GREAT. T. M. NO. 1491.; O. M. NOS. 767 and 770.

HOWFIELDS. A.D. 1609. Belonged to Westcott. Now a part of Great How Field.

HOWLS. A.D. 1609. Belonged to Hobby.

HUBBIN'S CLOSE. T. M. NO. 99 : O. M. NO. 100 (part of).

HULLE. A.D. 1219. Final concord at Westminster. Thomas de Hynedene tenant of two acres of land in Cocham, one of which lies upon Mitdene (Middons), and the other in the field called " Hulle ; " the same to Walter de Norfeld for an annual rent.

A.D. 1288. Final concord between Hugh Fitz Hugh de la Hulle and Hugh de la Hulle of a grant of land and messuage at Cocham for an annual payment of 1d., and a gift by Fitz Hugh of a sparrow-hawk. The Fitz Hughs succeeded the St. Quintins as Lords of the Manor of Bradleys, probably by marriage.

Hulle from *Hullus*, a hill (Martin).

HURSTREET. A.D. 1609. Francis Lord Norreys had land in Wellhouse field and in Hurstreet. Hurstreet probably led from the settlement at Wellhouse field to the great frith mentioned by Leland (Kerry) ; or it might be a continuation of Hurtestrete in Bray which led to the forest of Windsor.

A.D. 1325. John de Foxle seized of Hurtestrete in the forest of Windesore (Kerry).

Hurst, *E.*, from *hyrst*, a wood ; and strat, *E.*, from *stræte*, a way (Edm.).

HURTESTREET FURLONG. A.D. 1609. Mattingley had half an acre in Hurtestreet Furlong.

ICE LAKE. T. M. NO. 1091 ; O. M. NO. 673 (part of). Possibly isle or island ; the ground is swampy, and even now almost surrounded by water.

INCE, THE. T. M. NO. 39 ; O. M. NO. 89 (part of).

Probably a corruption of the Anglo-Saxon *hlinc*, a ridge of land left unploughed as a boundary in the open fields (Seebohm's " Village Communities ").

INWOOD. A.D. 1609. " Contains by estimation 120 acres. Sixty acres of which are severalled and enclosed, and the wood felled. And in the sixty acres unenclosed there is now little wood growing."

Inwood would probably have been exempt from the rights of the tenants, whether permanent or special, to fell timber, either for building, fencing, or firewood, until the large wood to the south of it— **Le Thickette**—had become exhausted of timber trees. When, to satisfy the acquired rights of the tenants, the Lord had to give up Inwood for this purpose, a rapid clearing of the timber, and, owing to an increased number of inhabitants, probably a larger quantity of cattle turned out to graze, would effectually prevent the growth of underwood ; the land becoming, and remaining, simply pasture ground. Whilst the timber having been felled more slowly on the Thickette a dense growth of underwood had followed, giving rise to the name.

The north or enclosed portion of Inwood remained coppice (*see* Coppice Farm) under the care of the Woodward, whose dwelling and small cleared holding lay immediately above and contiguous to it. And this coppice was probably the last charge of a manor official, whose post in earlier times must have been of no little importance.

A.D. 1287. Mast sold from Inwood for 9s. 9d. (Minist. Accts. Excheq.). *See* Cookham Dean Common.

IRLAS. *See* **Dyall Close.**

ISLIP EIOTT. An island in the Thames.

JOHN ATTE FIELDS. A.D. 1609. Godfrey had one acre called John atte Fields.

JOHN COPYHOLDS. A.D. 1509. John Willy elected collector for lands called John Copyholds (C. C. R.).

JOHN WISSES. A.D. 1508. Richard Babham elected collector for lands called John Wisses (C. C. R.).

JOHN'S CLOSE. T. M. NO. 1496 ; O. M. NO. 770 (part of).

JOHNSONS. A.D. 1525. Silvester Peck elected collector for lands called Johnsons (C. C. R.).

JORDANS LEAZE. A.D. 1609. Belonged to Babham.

JURDANS. A.D. 1493. Christopher Martin elected collector for lands called Jurdans (C. C. R.).

KAKESMEADE. A.D. 1609. Belonging to Bodley. Probably a corruption of Kitesmeade.

KAPDEN PITT. A.D. 1617. William Cutler settles on John Harding one acre in Kapden Pitt (private deed).

KENTISH DOWN BOTTOM. Part of Maidenhead Upper Field. NOS. 1676–85 ; O. M. NO. 96.
A.D. 1480. William Norreys is seized of lands called Bardolfs and Kents.

KENTS CHALK PIT. *See* Chalk Pit Kents.

KENTS DOWN. A.D. 1609. Belonged to Smith and Brice. Is now a part of Pinkneys.

KENTS, UPPER, MIDDLE, and LOWER. A.D. 1609. Part of Pinkneys.

KIDWELLS PARK. T. M. NO. 2160 ; O. M. NO. 177. *See* **Kymballs.**

KILN PLATT MEADOW, FIRST. T. M. NO. 914 ; O. M. NO. 229.

KILN PLATT MEADOW, SECOND. T. M. NO. 923 ; O. M. NO. 227.
So named from the brick and tile works carried on there by the Stevens. Richard Stevens, the son, after-

7

wards had the kiln at Pinkneys Green by Ditton House.

KING'S COPPICE FARM HOMESTEAD. T. M. NO. 858 ; O. M. NO. 50.

KITEFAIRE. A.D. 1609. Belonged to Hayes. This was near the Ray. Far, faire, *E.*, from *faer*, a way.

KITEFEARE. A.D. 1609. Belonged to Durdent.

KITES ACRE. A.D. 1609. Belonged to Brice.

KNIGHTWOOD. A.D. 1650. Ellington Wood alias Knightwood (Commonwealth Survey).

KYMBALLS. A.D. 1609. Belonged to Poole.
A.D. 1505. Alice Bukland left by her will to Sylvester Pecke a tenement called Kymballs.
Cwm, *B.*, a dingle ; bwla, *B.*, a bull (Edm.). *See* Kidwells.

LADY CLOSE. T. M. NO. 188 ; O. M. NO. 136.

LAKES, THE. T. M. NO. 1243 ; O. M. NO. 542. A low-lying meadow.

LANDGROVE. T. M. NO. 472 ; O. M. NO. 495. A part of Sutton Field abutting on Widbrook.

LANDSPITT. A.D. 1609. In the possession of Smith.

LANERLEAZE. A.D. 1482. Hedge broken at Lanerleaze (C. C. R.).

LANES LEAZE. A.D. 1609. Belonged to the Saracen's Head, or Tapster's property.
If the name be derived from land, *E.*, corruption of *len* or *laen*, it would signify land let out ; or, what is legally called fee farm land. If from lane, *D.*, *laan*, a lane or by-road, it would be the meadow next the lane. Or llan, *B.*, an enclosure ; læs, *E.*, a pasture (Edm.).

LANGDENE. A.D. 1527. A common field called Langdene (C. C. R.).

LANGDON, or GARGATE. A.D. 1609. Belonged to Durdent.

Lang, *E.*, long ; don or dun, *C.*, a hill (Edm.).

LANGROVE CLOSE. A.D. 1609. Part of Bullox. *See* Landgrove.

LANGTON'S CORNER. Part of Maidenhead Field. T. M. NO. 2029 ; O. M. Now the site of Garden Cottages. Name from the owners.

LANGTON'S FARM HOUSE. T. M. NO. 1334 ; O. M. NO. 532. Named probably from a former occupier. *See* Hindhay.

LANGTON'S SHAW. T. M. NO. 1340 ; O. M. NO. 540. *See* Langton's Farm.

LANKEY DOWN. *See* Linkey Down.

LATIMORE HOUSE. T. M. NOS. 2092 and 2093 ; O. M. NO. 1609.

Corruption of Lutman. A.D. 1609 Robert Lutman had a mansion house with a malt-house, barn, &c., near North Town. This house was afterwards the parish workhouse, and on the formation of the Cookham Union it was sold to James Darby, who about the year 1835 pulled it down and built the present house.

LAVELLYS, GREAT. T. M. NO. 174 ; O. M. NO. 90 (part of).

LAVELLYS, LITTLE. T. M. NO. 173 ; O. M. NO. 90 (part of). *See* **Laverleaze,** also Mabberley.

LAVERLEAZE. A.D. 1609. A part of Bradleys.

Laver, *E.*, from *hlaford*, lord, and leaze, *E.*, *lege*, meadow land (Edm.). *See* Lavellys.

LAVERMORE. A.D. 1609. A part of the Saracen's Head property.

LAWN FIELD. T. M. NOS. 1391 and 1392 ; O. M. NOS. 734, 735.

LAWRENCES. A.D. 1609. Belonged to the Dean and Chapter of Windsor.

LAWRENCES, LONG. A.D. 1609. Belonged to Westcott.

LAWRENCES, SHORT. A.D. 1609. Belonged to Westcott.

> The three Lawrences are now a part of How field.

LAYFIELD. A.D. 1609. A part of Harwoods. Now a part of Carter and Great Ley Field.

> Ley, *E.*, from *lege*, meadow.

LEA FARM. T. M. NO. 66 ; O. M. NO. 95. The Lea would seem to have been the chief manor court.

> A.D. 1371. Final concord in the King's Court at Cokham, held at La Leyhe before John Weche, Steward.
>
> A.D. 1371. Final agreement made at the King's Court at Cokham held at La Leyhe when Hugh of Berewyke (Braywick) releases to Robert le Baker, &c. (Bodleian deeds relating to Ray Mills).
>
> A.D. 1410. Final concord made in the Court of Sir Humphrey de Lancaster, the King's son, held at Legh in Cokham, James Lynde, Steward, &c.

LEAPFROG MEADOW. T. M. NOS. 1783 and 1784 ; O. M. NO. 641 (part of). ·

LEGG CROFT. A.D. 1609. Belonged to Nokes.

> Probably a corruption of Lea or Ley.

LEY, GREAT AND LITTLE. T. M. NO. 1276 ; O. M. NO. 565 (part of).

LEY, GREAT. A.D. 1609. Belonged to Weldon. *See* Ley Great.

LEY, LITTLE. A.D. 1609. Belonged to Weldon. *See* Ley, Little.

LEYS, GREAT. T. M. NO. 68 ; O. M. NO. 94.

LEYS GREEN. T. M. NO. 1230 ; O. M. NO. 621.

LICHTLOND. A.D. 1248. Grant to Simon de Passe-lewe of 5½ acres called Lichtlond (Charter Roll, Hen. 3rd). *See* **Lightlands.**

LICHTWUD. A.D. 1208. Grant to Adam, son of Ralph de Burnham, 5½ acres called Lichtwud (Charter Roll, 6 John).

LIGHTLANDS. T. M. NOS. between 589 and 614; O. M. NOS. 373 and 376.

A common arable field of 26 acres amongst 18 owners. It is sometimes called Littlelands, but as the holdings are not smaller than in other common fields, the name Littlelands, a modern one, arose probably from its contiguity to Small Mead.

A.D. 1553. Joan Ree, of Cookham, by will leaves to " Agnes Bristow, my naturel daughter, the yow in the light land sown at this time with wheat."

A.D. 1614. Will of Thomas Osbourne, of Cookham, " To my son Richard, one aker of otes in Light-lands." *See* **Litelands.**

LIGHTLANDS CLOSE. T. M. NO. 612 ; O. M. NO. 376.

LINKEY DOWN BOTTOM. T. M. NOS. between 1578 and 1634 ; O. M. NO. 641.

From Linch, a turf boundary between different ownerships in a common field.

LINKEY DOWN SHOT. In Maidenhead Field.

LION MEAD. T. M. NO. 2009 ; O. M. NO. 93. *See* Lyon.

LITELAKE CLOSE. A.D. 1609. Belonged to Weldon. *See* Dickerleys and the Lakes.

LITELANDS. A.D. 1609. A common arable field. It contained 42 acres amongst twelve owners.

A.D. 1205. John confirms to Adam, son of Ralf de Burneham, for his homage and service, one hide of land with the appurtenance in Cokham, and five acres and a half which are called Lichtwud, which William de Buggehazel held by the free service of one mark of silver per annum to be paid at the Feast of St. Michael and at Easter (Charter Roll, 6 John).

A.D. 1248. We have inspected and confirmed a charter which Gunild Kyrye made to Simon Passelewe for four score marks of silver in hand, of one hide of land with the appurtenances in Cokham, and five acres and a half of land which was called Lichtlond, which William Buggehazel formerly held by charter from King John to Adam de Burneham, whose heir I am (Charter Roll, 32 Hen. 3rd).

The name from licht, light, in Anglo-Saxon written liht (Earle), comes to it probably from some duty of providing rushes for lights, or perhaps the rushlights prepared. The land lies close to Bass Mead, where the rushes would be collected.

LITTLE CRANES. A.D. 1609. A part of Harwoods. *See* **Great Cranes.**

LITTLE GROVE. A.D. 1609. Part of Woodmancutts. *See* College, Little. ·

LITTLE MEAD. A.D. 1609. Part of Pinkneys.

LITTLE MEADOW. T. M. NO. 1792 ; O. M. NO. 651.

LITTLE SHEPHERD'S CLOSE. T. M. NO. 30 ; O. M. NO. 70.

LIXTON HILL. A.D. 1609. Belonged to Warner, Cherme, and Burley. Probably near to Broadcrofts.

LOCK MEAD. A.D. 1609. An area of 29½ acres amongst eight owners. Loc, *E.*, from loc or lucu, an enclosure (Edm.). *See* Lock Mead.

LOCK MEAD. T. M. NOS. between 1177 and 1187 ; O. M. NOS. 672 and 700. A common open meadow of 27 acres amongst six owners.

Before the cut at Boulter's Lock was made, the lock or sluice-gate was where the weir now is, and as it touched this meadow the name may probably have been due to this, or it might be a corruption of Lot Mead, as there was a custom of changing over the holdings from year to year at the time the land was severalled for hay-cutting.

A.D. 1650. It is called Locks Fields (Commonwealth Survey).

LOCK MEAD FOUR ACRES. T. M. NO. 1185; O. M. NO. 687.

LOCK MEAD FURLONG. T. M. NOS. between 1107 and 1128; O. M. NO. 661. Part of Lower Southey.

LOGGS CROFT. A.D. 1650. A certain place towards the west of Cookham Marsh called Loggs Croft (Commonwealth Survey).

LOLBROOK. A.D. 1609. That portion of the Lollybrook belonging to Bullox.

LOLLEBROOK. A.D. 1609. John Turner had a mansion house, &c., near the Brookside called Lollbrooks.

A.D. 1339. Ralf de Lulbrook conveys to William Trussel lands with pool, &c., at Lulbrook.

A.D. 1392. Thomas Nereis grants Reymulles to Thomas Lyllebrok.

A.D. 1592. William Weldon sells the mansion of Lullebrook to Thomas Turner.

Lol or Lul, probably from Lulla, the name of the Saxon lord (Edm.); Lollebrok from lollen, the murmuring or rippling brook (Kerry). *See* The Elms.

LOLLYBROOK. A backwater of the Thames from Cookham Ferry to the river at Babham's End. It forms a boundary to Odney.

LONG CLOSE. A.D. 1609. Bodley. Now T. M. NO. 1357.

LONG CLOSE. A.D. 1609. Harwoods. Now Bigfrith Shaw.

LONG CLOSE. A.D. 1609. Pinkneys. Now part of T. M. NO. 1383.

LONG CLOSE. A.D. 1609. Weldon. Now Long Close and Lower Long Close, Mount Farm. T. M. NOS. 1304 and 1305.

LONG CLOSE. A.D. 1609. Sharpe. Arable. It adjoined Cockmarsh.

LONG CLOSE. A.D. 1609. Bullox.

LONG CLOSE. T. M. NO. 1305 ; O. M. NO. 394.

LONG CLOSE, LOWER. T. M. NO. 1304 ; O. M. NO. 395.

LONG CLOSE, LOWER. T. M. NO. 1198 ; O. M. NO. 678.

LONG CROFT. A.D. 1609. Lawrences. Now a part of John's Close.

LONGDOWN. A.D. 1609. Woreston had land at Longdown.

LONG GROUND. T. M. NO. 863 ; O. M. NO. 206.

LONG LAKES CLOSE. A.D. 1609. Weldon. *See* Dickerleys and the Lakes.

LONGLEAZE. A.D. 1609. Saracen's Head. Now part of Dean Fields. T. M. NO. 1507.

LONGMEAD. A.D. 1609. Babham. *See* Fishery Meadow. T. M. NO. 402.

LONG MEAD. A.D. 1609. Bradleys. *See* Long Mead. T. M. NO. 31.

LONG MEAD. T. M. NO. 31 ; O. M. NO. 55.

LONG MEAD CLOSE. T. M. NO. 1198 ; O. M. NO. 678.

LONG MEAD HILL. T. M. NO. 403 ; O. M. NO. 480.

LONG MEAD TARR. An island in the River Thames.

LONG SHOT. T. M. NO. 1383 ; O. M. NO. 564 (part of).

LOT ACRE CLOSE. T. M. NO. 1375 ; O. M. NOS. 601 and 591 (part of).

LOT ACRE, GREAT. T. M. NO. 1374 ; O. M. NO. 591 (part of).

LOT ACRE, LITTLE. T. M. NO. 1373 ; O. M. NO. 590.
In digging gravel here flint implements have been found similar in character to those found in Ham

Field. Some of these are in the possession of Mr. Treacher, of Twyford, Berks.

Lot Acre, so called from the occupancy of the several plots being decided by lot drawing (Prothero).

LOUCHES. A.D. 1609. Belonged to Weldon.

A.D. 1392. William Louches is witness in a grant from Richard Martyn to John Mersshe, of Bray, of a messuage and four mills.

A.D. 1410. At a court held at La Legh, William Louches is a suitor (C. C. R.).

A.D. 1611. David Ray, yeoman, bequeaths his eldest son his messuage, &c., called Louches, " which I late bought of George Weldon."

Louch, from llwch, *E.*, a lake or pond (Edm.). The ground around Louches farm homestead, lying, as it does, just below Mount Hill, is full of water, and probably a spot where there was formerly a lake or pool in the ancient woods. This may have been the inducement for clearing and erecting a homestead. *See* Louches Farm.

LOUCHES FARM HOMESTEAD. T. M. NOS. 1309 and 1310; O. M. NO. 270. *See* **Louches.**

LOUSY HILL. T. M. NOS. between 1646 and 1711; O. M. NO. 638.

Will this name have any connection with the family of Louisey? *See* **Belton's Barn.**

LOUSY HILL CLOSE. T. M. NO. 1639; O. M. NO. 638.

LOVE LANE. T. M. NO. 146 ; O. M. NOS. 135 and 136 (part of).

LOVES CLOSE. A.D. 1609. Belonged to Godfrey.

LOVESLOND. A.D. 1509. Close of pasture called Loveslond (C. C. R.).

LOWEBROKE. A.D. 1508. Presentment that the bridge is broken at Lowebroke (C. C. R.).

8

LOWER DEAN CLOSE. A.D. 1609. Belonged to Nokes; it was near to Hall Dore.

LOWER FIELD CLOSE. A.D. 1609. Bodley. Now Lower Field.

LOWER FIELD. T. M. NOS. 1371 and 1372; O. M. NO. 598.

LOWER GROUND. T. M. NOS. 1174 and 1175; O. M. NO. 672.

LUDLOWS. A.D. 1609. Three closes belonging to Wynch.

A.D. 1412. Thomas Whyte grants to John Lawrence reversion of lands which Margaret, wife of Richard Lodelaw, holds in dower.

A.D. 1489. William Danvers, Justice of the King's Bench, and John Wells, ought to repair their hedges by the common way lying between their lands, called Mores and Ludlows.

A.D. 1541. Suitors elect George Ludlowe collector for lands called Pynkneys (C. C. R.).

A.D. 1545. George Ludlowe sells Thomas Weldon the Manor of Pynkneys (C. C. R.).

LUFFENHAM. A.D. 1609. Belongs to Babham.

A.D. 1423. John Luffenham, of Corryrvell, bequeaths "to Henry Messenger my house in Cookham" (Will of John Luffenham).

Luffen, from Lufan, a Saxon lord (Edm.).

LULLEBROK. A.D. 1208. *See* **Lollybroke.**

LYON. A.D. 1609. At North Town, belongs to Herbert. *See* Lion Mead.

LYON, THE. A.D. 1609. At Maidenhead, belongs to Peck.

A.D. 1489. William Maynard keeps a certain inn called the Lyon (C. C. R.).

A.D. 1495. Geoffrey Mayle keeps a certain inn called the Lyon (C. C. R.).

MABBERLEY, GREAT. *See* Lavellys.

MABBERLEY, LITTLE. *See* Lavellys.

MAIDENHEAD FIELDS. A.D. 1609. Arable common fields with an area, including North Town Fields, of 368 acres amongst twenty-three owners.

MAIDENHEAD FIELDS. T. M. NOS. between 1556 and 2157 ; O. M. NOS. between 45 and 639. Upper Middle and Lower (the Lower being North Town Fields) have an area of 290 acres in 217 lots amongst seventeen owners. This shows that a considerable area had been enclosed since 1609.

MAIDENHEAD, THE VILLAGE OF. A.D. 1609. The wording runs thus ; " The Guardian, Burgess, and Common Council of the Village of Maidenhead." The term village may probably be accounted for in that Maidenhead was not a distinct parish. It lies partly in Cookham, partly in Bray, these parishes being separated by the London and Western Road, of which the main street of Maidenhead forms a part ; Cookham lies on the north, Bray on the south. The name of Maidenhead has given rise to the myth that here was buried the head of one of the eleven thousand martyred Virgins of Cologne. And this Cologne legend of St. Ursula seems to have arisen from a clerical error in the calendar, by which the name of St. Undecemilla, virgin martyr, appears as Undecem millia Virg. Mart. But " Maidenhythe, the ancient form of the name, shows that it was the midway wharf between Marlow and Windsor " (Isaac Taylor).

" Maidenhead, *E.*, corrupted from Maidenhithe, the Virgin Mary's port " (Edm.).

The late Colonel Cooper King, in his ' History of Berkshire,' says it was " called Maidenhuth in the year 1288, and Maydenhead in the year 1500. Partly derived from ' hithe ' a wharf for timber. It may have been also partly derived from the

Mai dun or great hill of Taplow on the opposite bank."

Maidenhead was, in the year 1895, formed into a distinct parish.

MAIDENHEAD LANE. *See* Six Acres, Maidenhead Lane.

MALDERS LANE. T. M. NO. 1278 ; O. M. NO. 566. Formerly Nelders.

MALDONS. A.D. 1672. A part of Cannon Court called Maldons. *See* Malders Lane.

MARLOW ROAD SHOT. T. M. NO. 1672 ; O. M. NO. 45. A part of Maidenhead Field.

MARFIELD. A.D. 1609. Belonged to Godfrey.

MARLSTON. A.D. 1536. Lionel Norris to Humphry Clery a messuage called Marlston.

MARSH MEADOW. A.D. 1609. A common meadow of 29 acres divided amongst nine owners.

Mar, *E.*, from *mere*, a pool (Edm.). *See* Marsh Cookham.

MARSH COOKHAM. T. M. NOS. 218 to 233 ; O. M. NOS. 165 to 168.

A meadow with an area of 31 acres amongst nine owners, who held it in severalty for the hay-crop, and then in common of pasturage proportionately to the size of their ownerships.

MEADE. *See* Small Meade.

MEAD HILL. T. M. NO. 1257 ; O. M. NO. 592.

MEAD HILL, GREAT. T. M. NOS. 986 and 1257 ; O. M. NO. 415 (part of).

MEAD HILL, LITTLE. T. M. NO. 987 ; O. M. NO. 415 (part of).

MEADOW, LITTLE. A.D. 1609. Ground adjoining Cockmarsh Hill, owned by Sharpe.

MEREWORTH. A.D. 1456. Tenants elected to the office of collector for Mereworth (C. C. R.).

MERSSHEMEDE ACRE. A.D. 1510. Taking cattle from a place called Mersshemede Acre (C. C. R.).

MICHEN MEADE. A.D. 1609. Part of Bradleys.

> Mich, *E.*, from mycel, great (Edm.). *See* Minson Meadow.

MICHEN MEADE EIGHT. An island belonging to Bradleys.

MIDDONS, GREAT. A.D. 1609. Belonged to Farmer and Sharpe.

> Either from Mid, *E.*, middle, or Met, *E.*, from metan to measure, and Den, enclosure. *See* Bradcutts T. M. NO. 322.

MIDDONS, LITTLE. A.D. 1609. The three closes adjoining Patches Grove which belonged to Sharpe. *See* the Three Closes.

MIDDONS, MIDDLE. A.D. 1609. Belonged to Farmer. *See* Little Shepherds Close.

MILES PLATT. T. M. NO. 1441 ; O. M. NO. 737.

MILKHEGGE. A.D. 1456. A hedge broken at Milkhegge (C. C. R.).

MILL CLOSE. A.D. 1609. Belonged to Westcott.

MILL EYOTT, and BIRDS CLOSE. T. M. NO. 353 ; O. M. NO. 421.

> A water-mill had formerly been there. The course of the mill-stream, though now filled in, is still to be traced. *See* Birds Close.

MINSON MEADOW. T. M. NO. 178 ; O. M. NO. 90. *See* **Michen Meade.**

MONKEDONS. A.D. 1609. Belonged to Poole. Named from its former owners, to one of whom there is a monumental brass in Cookham Church.

A.D. 1712. Austin is collector for Munkington.

MOORES. A.D. 1609. Part of Saracen's Head property. Named from the family of More or Atte More in Bray.

A.D. 1358. John atte More held lands in Cokham.

A.D. 1395. Thomas atte More tenant of Cookham Manor.

A.D. 1395. William atte More of Cokham paid 4*d.* for keeping his pigs in the King's Meadow (Kerry Bray).

A.D. 1489. William Danvers and John Wills ought to repair their hedges by the common way lying between their lands called Mores and Ludlows (C. C. R.).

MOOR HALL. T. M. NO. 278 ; O. M. NO. 355. Adjoins to Cookham Moor.

MOOR HALL MEADOWS. T. M. NOS. 523, 551, and 568 ; O. M. NOS. 375 and 356.

MOOR LANE PIECE. T. M. NO. 1970 ; O. M. NO. 220 (part of).

MORE CROFT. A.D. 1649. A meadow, lying near Widbrooke pasture, called Morecroft.

MORIS LANE. A.D. 1514. An order to scour Moris Lane (C. C. R.).

MOSSY HILL. T. M. NOS. 1722 and 1732 ; O. M. NOS. 608 and 609 (part of).

MOSSY HILL SHOT. Part of Wellhouse Field. T. M. NOS. 1721 and 1723 ; O. M. NO. 640 (part of).

MOULDERS. T. M. NO. 1294 ; O. M. NO. 565 (part of). Formerly Nelders.

MOULDERS LANE. Also Malders Lane.

MOUNT FARM. T. M. NO. 979 ; O. M. NO. 392. Formerly Harwoods.

MOUNT FIELD. T. M. NO. 973 ; O. M. NO. 257 (part of).

MOUNT HILL. O. M. NO. 257 (part of).

On the south side of Mount Hill are several terraces, evidently artificial, and which one can hardly understand to have been made for defensive purposes. These, in the opinion of the late Mr.

Gordon Hills, were the site of a vineyard, most probably Roman.

MULLEYTES. A.D. 1322. Decay of a certain island called Mulleytes (Minist. Accts., 15 Edw., 2nd).

MUNKEAMS. A.D. 1514. Lands in Maidenhead and Cokham called Munkeams (C. C. R.).

MUSHHORN. A.D. 1711. Whitfield appointed collector for lands called Mushhorn.

MYLLE GARDEN. A.D. 1483. Common way not repaired between Myllegarden and Myllemede (C. C. R.).

NAPKIN PITTS. A.D. 1609. Belonged to Poole.
Knap, *B.*, from *cnap*, a round, isolated hill (Edm.).

NAVELLING PITS. T. M. NOS. 688 and 690; O. M. NO. 365 (part of).
Naven, *E.*, from *nafa*, the middle; Ing., *E.*, meadow (Edm.). It lays in the middle of the south end of Ham Field.

NEATS CROPS. T. M. NO. 28; O. M. NO 65. A corruption of Reycrofts. It was formerly **Reycrofts Meadow.**

NELDERS. A.D. 1609. Belonged to Weldon; is now Moulders.

NEW CLOSE. A.D. 1609. In Sherling and belonged to Turner.

NEW EIOTT. An island in the River Thames.

NEW LEAZE. A.D. 1609. Part of Pinkneys. Probably a part of Longshot.

NEWMANS. A.D. 1705. Robert Ray appointed collector for Newmans. Newmans belonged to Noah Barnard, who in the year 1692 was buried in Cookham Church. (T. M. NO. 299; O. M. The smithy and dwelling-house belonging to Mr. Lane. (This was part of Newmans.)

NIDDON. A.D. 1477. A hedge broken at Niddon (C. C. R.).

NOAH'S ARK. A part of Rowborrow. When the railway cutting was made old weapons and some skeletons were unearthed there. Noah Barnard had land in Rowborrow and the name may be a corruption of Noah's balk or boundary. His holding may possibly be identified.

NORTH MOOR. T. M. NO. 1232 ; O. M. NO. 620.

Here are some well-defined earthworks. In the year 1886 Mr. Rutland examined them and in the centre discovered what had been a well 2 ft. 2 in. in diameter. In it he found a quantity of bones, broken pottery, and fragments of roofing tiles. The pottery and tiles were Roman or Romano-British. North Moor is a meadow surrounded by water save at a portion of the west side where was the entrance to the entrenchments. Its situation and character warrant the inference that the Manor of Ellington obtained its name here ; Ey, island ; Ing, meadow ; Ton, settlement. The earthworks prove it to have been, at all events, a military settlement ; and it is a meadow fenced in by water. This fortification may have had some connection with the large Romano-British settlement of Wellhousefield.

NORTH TOWN CLOSE. A.D. 1609. Belonged to Poole. It probably is now North Town Meadow.

NORTH TOWN FIELD. A.D. 1609. Was an arable common field with an area of 45 acres amongst eleven owners. *See* Maidenhead Fields.

North Town, a part of Knight Ellington, probably acquired the name from its relative position to Maidenhead or *South* Ellington.

NORTH TOWN MEADE. A.D. 1609. Belonged to Pinkneys and is now a part of Feens Moor.

NORTH TOWN PIGHTLE. A.D. 1609. Part of Saracen's Head property.

NORTH TOWN FIELDS. *See* Maidenhead Fields.

NORTH TOWN MEADOW. T. M. NO. 2008 and 2013; O. M. NO. 86.

NORTH TOWN MOOR. T. M. NO. 1803; O. M. NO. 633.

NORTH TOWN PIECE. T. M. NOS. 2060 and 2071; O. M. NO. 82 (south part of).

NUNPITT FERE. A.D. 1609. Belonged to Sharpe.

NUTTINGS FARM. T. M. NO. 34; O. M. NO. 73. If this be an ancient name, it probably is derived from Nets, *E.*, from *næt.*, cattle, and Ing, *E.*, meadow.

OAKEN GROVE. A.D. 1609. Part of Pinkneys. *See* Oaken Grove.

OAKEN GROVE. A.D. 1609. Part of Weldons. *See* Beechen Grove. T. M. NO. 1300.

OAKEN GROVE. T. M. NO. 1382; O. M. NO. 634.

OAKLEY CLOSE. T. M. NOS. 607 and 608; O. M. NO. 386 (part of).

OAKLEY CLOSE UNDER. T. M. NOS. 609 and 611; O. M. NO. 386.

OAKLEY HEDGE CLOSES. A.D. 1609. Belonged to Readings. Was probably that now Oakley Close.

ODNEY. A.D. 1609. Babhams had land in Odney.

An island bounded by a short piece of the main river on the east, but mostly by two streams issuing from the river Thames at Cookham Ferry, and joining the main stream again opposite Cliefden Woods. The one stream dividing Odney from Sasshes; the other being the Lollybrook, which re-enters the Thames at Babham End. The area of Odney is nearly seventy acres. Odney acquires its name from Odin, the Danish war god, and eye, an island. To Odin the island was probably sacred. When the cut was being made through Sasshes, a quantity of

9

weapons said to be Danish were discovered near to where the pound lock now is.

ODNEY GREEN. A.D. 1609. By estimation seven acres. A common of pasture to the inhabitants all the year.

A.D. 1483. William Wallington, tithing man for Odney.

A.D. 1488. Richard Wykes, tithing man for Odenhey, presents that Richard Decon overburdens the pasture at Odenhey Green (C. C. R.).

A.D. 1493. William Norys bequeaths lands at Odney, occupied by Andrew Banbury, to William Babham. (Will of William Noreys.) *See* Odney Common.

ODNEY CLOSE. A.D. 1609. Belongs to Babham.

A.D. 1588. Roger Osbourne leaves to his son John Osbourne a close called Odneys Close. (Will of Roger Osbourne).

ODNEY, GREAT. A.D. 1609. Part of Bullox.

ODNEY, LITTLE. A.D. 1609. Part of Babhams. Now Birds Close.

ODNEY COMMON. T. M. NO. 349; O. M. NOS. 425 and 426.

Common of pasturage to the inhabitants. In area 7¾ acres.

OLDEBURY. A.D. 1415. Land bequeathed by William Louch at Oldebury. Oldebury or Aldebury, in contra-distinction to the Viccaridge Bury.

OLDEFIELD. A.D. 1543. Richard Neve has placed a mangy mare in the field called *Oldefield* (C. C. R.).

OLDE HOUSE GREEN. A.D. 1609. Is now called Bowdens Green.

A.D. 1706. John Hamerton sells John Dodson the Dean Close Piddle, abutting on a lane called Broadcroft Lane, leading from *Old House Green* towards Maidenhead. (Private Doc.) *See* Dyall Close.

OLDE LEYS. A.D. 1488. Will South trespasses on a close at Le Rey called Olde Leys (C. C. R.). Probably Holman Leaze.

OMMAN LEAZE. T. M. NOS. 2026 and 2027 ; O. M. NOS. 129 and 134. *See* Holman Leaze also.

OMMAN LEAZE MEADOW. T. M. NOS. 2024 and 2025 ; O. M. NOS. 129 and 134.

OMMAN LEAZE SHOT. T. M. NOS. between 1985 and 1996 ; O. M. NO. 183. Part of Ray Field.

OSBORNES. A.D. 1511. Lands sometimes called Osbornes (C. C. R.).

OVEYS or COOKHAM TOWN FARM. From a former occupant.

A.D. 1731. Mr. Terry paid land tax of 1*l.* 10*s.* on Woveys.

A.D. 1759. Cooks or Hamertons, formerly occupied by Rich. Terry ; before him by Rich. Ovey.

Roland Hynde held the manor of Oveys. Private Docs.).

OXEN CLOSE. T. M. NOS. 2254 and 2257 : O. M. East St. Cottages, thence to the Cookham Road.

OXNEYS MEAD. T. M. NO. 1186 ; O. M. NOS. 684 and 685.

PAGES WHARF. A.D. 1634. Near Babham Lea. (Min. Accts. Exch.)

PARK, THE. A.D. 1609. Near Terris Grove.

PARKERS FIELD. T. M. NO. 1401 ; O. M. NO. 732.

PARSONS CROFT. A.D. 1609. Part of Readings.

A.D. 1634. One croft, called Parsons Croft, late in the occupation of Thos. Babham.

PARSONS CROFT. T. M. NO. 102 ; O. M. NO. 163 (part of).

PARTRIDGE MEAD. T. M. NO. 1237 ; O. M. NO. 620.

PASSINGHAMS. A.D. 1494. Pecke collector for lands called Passinghams (C. C. R.).

PATCHES CLOSE. T. M. NOS. 25 and 26; O. M. NO. 69.

PATCHES WOOD. T. M. NOS. 23 and 24; O. M. NO. 69. *See* **Patches Grove.**

PATCHES GROVE. A.D. 1609. Belonged to Sharpe. Is now Patches Wood.

PAULS FOOT. T. M. NO. 1131; O. M. NO. 672.

PAULS LEG. T. M. NO. 1132; O. M. NO. 671.

PEACOCKS TARR. An island in the Thames.

PEAKED BALD STEYS. *See* Bald Steys.

PEAKED CLOSE. T. M. NO. 1098; O. M. NO. 322.

PEAKED CLOSE. T. M. NO. 658; O. M. NO. 382.

PEAKED CLOSE. T. M. NO. 751; O. M. NO. 310.

PEAKED PIECE. T. M. NO. 1551; O. M. NO. 332.

PEDILLS. A.D. 1509. A pasture called Pedills.
A.D. 1552. Robert Kember had a house called Pedills (C. C. R.).

PENLING CLOSE. T. M. NOS. 630 and 633 : O. M. NO. 385.

PENNYFADERS. A.D. 1609. Belonged to Austin.
A.D. 1650. William Aston paid 10s. for Pennyfathers. Land some time in the tenure of George Washington.

PENNYFEATHERS. A.D. 1656. In or abutting on Pound Field.

PERRYCROFT. A.D. 1609. Belonged to Babham.
A.D. 1647. Noah Barnard bequeaths to his wife Phillis Barnard "two long ackers butting upon Perycroft." *See* Perrycroft.

PERRYCROFT. T. M. NO. 409; O. M. NO. 475.

PERRYCROFT MEADOW. T. M. NO. 340; O. M. NO. 475.

PETER'S CLOSE. T. M. NO. 823 ; O. M. NO. 109.

PHILBYS. T. M. NO. 750 ; O. M. NO. 310. *See* Filbys.
A.D. 1731. John Bennett rented Philbys (Priv. Doc.).

PICKED CLOSE. A.D. 1609. Part of Pinkneys.
Now part of Great Bartleys.

PICKED CLOSE. A.D. 1609. Pecks.

PICKED CLOSE. A.D. 1609. Rays. Now part of
O. M. NO. 310.

PICKED CLOSE. A.D. 1609. Smiths.

PICKED FERE. A.D. 1609. Pinkneys. Now probably part of Oaken Grove. Fere. *E., frer.* a way.

PICKSFIELD CLOSE. T. M. NO. 999 ; O. M. NO. 571
(part of).

PIGEON HOUSE CLOSE. T. M. NO. 468 : O. M. NO.
479 (part of).

PIGEON HOUSE COPPICE. A.D. 1609. Part of
Harwoods. *See* Pigeon House Wood.

PIGEON HOUSE COPPICE. T. M. NO. 969 : O. M.
NO. 257.

PIGEON HOUSE WOOD. T. M. NO. 967 : O. M. NO.
265. Formerly PIGEON HOUSE COPPICE.

PINKNEYS FARM HOMESTEAD. T. M. NO. 1363 :
O. M. NO. 557.

PINKNEYS GREEN. T. M. NO. 1318 ; O. M. NO. 526.
A common of pasturage to the tenants of the Manor ;
in area about 170 acres.
A.D. 1609. It formed a part of Inwood.

PINKNEYS HILL. A.D. 1609. Part of Pinkneys
(Exch. Inquir.).
A.D. 1636. Pinkneys Hill or Worthy lies within the
liberty of Knight Ellington, and William Mattingley
was presented for altering a Church path through
Pinkneys Hill (C. C. R.).

PINKNEYS HILL, INNER. T. M. NO. 1370; O. M. NO. 597.

PINKNEYS HILL, LOWER. T. M. NO. 1369; O. M. NO. 599.

PINKNEYS HILL, UPPER. T. M. NO. 1367; O. M. NO. 599. Formerly **BARDEL DOWN.**

PINKNEYS HOUSE. T. M. NO. 1393; O. M. NO. 563. Now Clarefield. Pinkneys acquired its name from the Pinkenni family.

A.D. 1393. John Pinkeny becomes the possessor of lands in Cookham, which, with others subsequently acquired, remained to the Pynkenys until A.D. 1459, when Agnes, the widow of John Pynkney, but then the wife of John Appurley, sells the whole of them to Robert Beaumont, clerk (Feet of Fines).

The Pinkeny family were, however, connected with Cookham parish prior to this purchase of 1393 ; for A.D. 1198 Simon de Pinkenni grants to Simon de Pinkenni, his nephew, a virgate of land in Helingeton (Rot. Cur. Regis.).

A.D. 1409. Inquest taken at Waltham St. Lawrence ; the jurors find that Arnold Pynkeny held of the King-in-Chief, on the day he died, the Manor called Pynkeny Place, within the Parish of Cookham. (There is a monumental brass in Cookham Church to Arnold Pynkenni dated A.D. 1402.)

A.D. 1480. William Norreys and Roger Bulstrode were seized of the Manor of Pynkennys.

A.D. 1545. George Ludlow sells Thomas Weldon the Manor of Pinkenys.

PITFIELDS. T. M. NO. 1269; O. M. NO. 567. *See* **Pixfield Close.**

PIXFIELD CLOSE. A.D. 1609. Belonged to Turner.

A.D. 1581. Roger Lutman bequeathed a close of Pasture called Pixfield to his son. *See* Pitfields.

PLACE ORCHARD. T. M. NO. 968; O. M. NO. 266. The foundations of old buildings found on this ground point to its being the site of Harwood's Manor House. According to the survey of A.D. 1609 there were attached to the Manor House 6 acres of land and 52 acres of warren land, which, or the most of it, would probably have been on Mount Hill.

PLAISTERS. A.D. 1609. Belonged to Bullox.

A.D. 1731. John Bennett rented Plasters (Priv. Doc.).

Plaistow, Plestor, *E.*, from play and stow, the enclosure for play or public recreation ground (Edm.).

Plaisters lies alongside the highway, and, besides the Dean, is close to Ham Field as well as to Soane's, Filby's, and Bughazel's, all names which indicate the existence in early times of habitations ; and this may explain the reason for the setting aside of a portion of ground for military exercise and practice. *See* Plastows.

PLASTOWS. T. M. NO. 716 ; O. M. NO. 310. The north-east corner of this field was formerly a separate coppice belonging to John Sawyer, of Cookham, and known as Dean Close Piddle. *See* **Plaisters.**

PLATT. A.D. 1609. An enclosure of Lammas land belonging to Westcott called Platt.

POND MEAD. T. M. NOS. 2018, 2019 ; O. M. NO. 89.

POOR MAN A PENY. T. M. NO. 1552 ; O. M. NO. 142 (part of).

POPES LANE. A highway leading between O. M. NOS. 151 and 154. In Bingley's Map it is named Hopps Lane.

POULTON MEAD. T. M. NOS. 1825 to 1922 ; O. M. NOS. between 25 and 691. A common meadow with an area of 41½ acres in twenty-five portions amongst fourteen owners. The north-westerly portion is low-lying swampy ground. Formerly it

was known as Fulpole Mead and Fulton Mead ;
after that as Fountain Mead. *See* Fountain Mead.

POULTON MEAD SHOT. A part of Ray Field.

POUND CLOSE. A.D. 1609. Belonged to Pecke.

POUND CLOSE. T. M. NOS. 474, 655, 656, 657 ;
O. M. NOS. 366, 490. *

POUND CORNER. T. M. NOS. between 449 and 458 ;
O. M. NO. 490.

POUND FARM. T. M. NO. 214 ; O. M. NO 343.

POUND FIELD. A.D. 1609. Arable land comprising 134 acres amongst twenty-one owners. The
Pound fields were in different parts of the parish,
and adjacent to the several Manor Pounds.

POUND FIELD. T. M. NO. 1457 ; O. M. NOS. 714,
715.

POUND FIELD. T. M. NOS. 110 to 145 ; O. M. NOS.
between 163 and 336.

POUND FIELD. T. M. NOS. 191 to 194 ; O. M. NOS.
287, 339, 340. Arable fields in area 68½ acres
amongst ten owners.

POUND FIELD, GREAT. T. M. NO. 1260 ; O. M. NO.
591.

POUND FIELD, LITTLE. T. M. NO. 1258 ; O. M. NO.
591.

POUND FIELD, LONG. T. M. NO. 1259 ; O. M. NO.
591.

POUND FIELD, PIGHTLE. T. M. NOS. 125 and 126.
O. M. NO. 336.

POUND FIELD HILL. A.D. 1609. Belonged to
Nokes.

PRIEST MEADE. A.D. 1609. Belonged to Weldon.
Pris *E.*, from presbyter (Edm.).

PRESS MEADE FURLONG. Part of Sutton Field.
T. M. NO. 503 ; O. M. NO. 411.

PRIORS LEZE. A.D. 1561. Arthur Babham owned a close called Priors Leze (Cookham Wills). Now a part of Formosa or Odney Meadow. O. M. NO. 429.

PUDDING ACRE. T. M. NOS. between 410 and 416; O. M. NOS. 470 and 474.

PUDSEYS. T. M. NO. 926; O. M. NOS. 247, 248.
A.D. 1758. This was owned by Thomas Pudsey, of Cookham Dean, who was by trade a higler (Priv. Doc.).

PUNTALLS COPPICE. T. M. NO. 975; O. M. NO. 390.

PUNT HILL. T. M. NO. 1502; O. M. NO. 779.

QUANGUINS OAK. A.D. 1609. Bullox. In Pound Field.

QUEENS COMMON. A.D. 1524. A part of Great Bradleys (C. C. R.).

QUEENS EIOTT. An island in the river Thames.

RAGABACK CLOSE. T. M. NO. 801; O. M. NO. 147.
Rag *E.*, rugged; back *E.*, from *bac*, a ridge (Edm.). This is a fair description of the ground.

RANDALLS. A.D. 1609. Part of Pinkneys.

RANDALLS. T. M. NO. 1489; O. M. NO. 760.

RAWLINGS, LITTLE. T. M. NO. 1802; O. M. NO. 653.
Raw, *E.*, from *ruh*, rough; ing, *E.*, meadow.

RAY FIELD. A.D. 1609. A common arable field in area 207 acres amongst twenty owners.
An ancient riverside settlement, it derives its name from the connection with the river.
Ray or Rey, *E.*, from *ree*, a stream (Edm.).

RAY FIELD. T. M. NOS. from 1808; O. M. NOS. 22, 23, 24, and between 211 and 228.
A common arable field of 133 acres divided into 115 portions amongst fourteen owners.
For a long period the Rays, who acquired their

name from this locality, were an important yeoman and trading family in the parish. The earliest of them, of whom mention is made, being John de la Reye, whose son Alexander atte Rey grants a lease of Ray Mills in the year 1346 to Hugh of Berewyke. The last one Richard Ray was up to the year 1783 a brewer in Cookham. *See* **Ray Mills** and **Ray Field**.

RAY MILLS. A.D. 1609. The property of Sir Thomas Bodley, who in that same year presents it, with other properties, to the University of Oxford.

 A.D. 1346. A lease from Alexander atte Reye, Nicolas atte Reye, and other children of John de la Reye to Hugh of Berewyke (Braywick) of a messuage and lands in Cokham.

 A.D. 1347. Indenture between Hugh Berewyke and Nicolas atte Reye, of Cokham, as to the mills called *Rey mulles* in Cokham.

 A.D. 1369. Hugh, of Berewyke, releases to Robert le Bakere, of Braye, all lands and mills in Cokham late of John atte Reye.

 A.D. 1371. This grant is confirmed at the King's Court at Cokham, held at La Legh.

 A.D. 1392. Thomas Norreys name appears in connection with this property, and it remained with his family until it was sold to Sir Thomas Bodley (Docum. Bodl. Library).

RAY MILL CLOSE. A.D. 1609. Belonged to Pecke.

READINGS CLOSE. A.D. 1609. Belonged to Bodley. **Readings** formerly **Redische.**

READINGS FIELD. T. M. NO. 770 ; O. M. NO. 154.

REDDOWAY'S LITTLE. T. M. NO. 94 ; O. M. NO. 159. Named from a former owner.

REDISCHE. The manor or farm of Hendons was also called Redisches farm (Bodl. Deeds).

REYCROFTS. A.D. 1609. A part of Bradleys. It was the Rey or river Croft. The ground adjoins the river,

A.D. 1488. Will. South entered the close of John Pury at le Rey in le olde Leys (La Legh), and consumed the grass with his animals (C. C. R.).

Reycrofts is now Neatcrops.

REYCROFTS COPPICE. A.D. 1609 Part of Bradleys.

Reycrofts Coppice or the coppice of the river Croft is now corrupted into Spots Mead.

RICKSFIELD. T. M. NO. 1000 ; O. M. NO. 571.

RIDINGS. *See* Shepherd's Field.

ROAD FURLONG. T. M. NO. 1159 ; O. M. NO. 663. Part of Sutton Field.

ROCKETT. A.D. 1609. An open common estimated to be 20 acres in extent. It was a part of Bigfrith.

ROOKHILL. T. M. NOS. 988 to 992 ; O. M. NO. 415.

ROOKHILL ENCLOSED. T. M. NO. 1254 ; O. M. NO. 415.

ROUGH MEAD. T. M. NO. 1001 ; O. M. NO. 576. Formerly **Rowmede.**

ROUND COPPICE. T. M. NO. 59 ; O. M. NO. 98.

ROWBORROW. A.D. 1609. An arable common field of 147½ acres divided amongst fifteen owners.

Row, *E.*, from *ruh*, rough or uncultivated ; borrow, from burgh, *E.*, *buhr*, a fortified hill. *See* Rowborrow.

ROWBORROW. T. M. NOS. within 152 and 187 ; O. M. NOS. between 89 and 136. An area of 66¼ acres divided into twenty-seven portions amongst eight owners.

When the cutting for the Wycombe railway was made through Rowborrow—iron implements, and other relics of the Anglo-Saxon period were unearthed, as well as several skeletons. A description of these is published in vol. xv of the 'Archæological Journal.' *See* **Rowborrow.**

ROWMEDE. A.D. 1609. It belonged to Weldon.

A.D. 1511. The meadow of Rowmede occurs (C. C. R.). Now Rough Mead.

SALISBURY QUARRY. A.D. 1502. A drain not made in Salisbury Quarry (C. C. R.).

The large pit in Bisham Wood in which Quarry Cottage is built.

SANDHILL CLOSE. T. M. NO. 1834 ; O. M. NO. 242. Now Horton Grange.

Houses built on Sandhill Close, at the beginning of this century, failing occupants on account of their situation, were pulled down and the materials used for building the two houses at the north corner of Blackamore Lane, on the main road from Maidenhead to Cookham.

SANDHILL FIELD. T. M. NO. 1876 ; O. M. NO. 243.

SARACENS HEAD. A.D. 1609. This property belonged to Thomas Waller.

A.D. 1563. It was owned by Thomas Weldon.

SASHES. O. M. NOS. 193 and 203. The navigation cut, shortening the waterway of the river Thames, passes through Sashes. When it was made a number of skeletons with Roman swords and javelin heads were found (Records of Buckinghamshire). In the year 1893, when constructing a boat slide to the Pound in Sasshes, the remains of a pile dwelling with bones and broken pottery were discovered. They are described by Mr. Goolden in the April number of the ' Berks. Arch. Soc. Journ.' of that year. Some of these are in the Reading Museum. *See* **Shawses.**

SCHRINGING OKE. A.D. 1554. Bequest of 2 akers of barly lying in Schringing oke (will of Alice Cutler).

SEWIS. A.D. 1495. Lands called Sewis (C. C. R.).

SHACKLES MOOR. T. M. NO. 1490 ; O. M. NO. 767.

SHAFTSEYS EIGHT. An Island in the Thames, near to Sashes.

SHASSES. A.D. 1577. Occurs on Monument to Raffe More in Cookham Church. *See* Sashes.

SHAWSES. A.D. 1609. Part of Bullox.

From Sceole, a shoal and eye island (Edm.). It is an island bounded partly by the main stream of the Thames and partly by a backwater, the latter dividing it from Odney. It is evidently formed by the silting up of the ground as the river struck against the hill on the opposite side.

Its proximity to Odney also suggests Ceols-eye as derived from Ceolwulf, from whom Cholseye and Chelseye acquired their names (Cooper King's Berks). *See* Sashes.

SHAWES WATER. A.D. 1609. Belonged to Dorothy Fitzwilliam.

SHEARLAND CLOSE. T. M. NO. 1211 ; O. M. NO. 595.

SHEARLINGS. T. M. NO. 1007 ; O. M. NO. 663.

SHEEPHOUSE FARM HOUSE. T. M. NO. 1189 ; O. M. NO. 681.

The earlier name was Ship house, indicating some connection with the boat traffic on the river. *See* **Shiphouse.**

SHEEPHOUSE CLOSE. T. M. NO. 1192 ; O. M. NO. 683 (part of).

SHEEPCOTT. A.D. 1609. Part of Pinkneys. Now a portion of Oaken Grove.

SHEEPLEAZE. A.D. 1609. Part of Bradleys.

SHEPHERDS CLOSE. A.D. 1609. Belonged to Weldon.

SHEPHERDS CLOSE, LITTLE. T. M. NO. 30 ; O. M. NO. 70.

SHEPHERDS COPPICE. A.D. 1609. Belonged to Weldon. *See* **Windmill field Coppice,** now Windmill Shaw.

SHEPHERDS FIELD and RIDINGS. T. M. NO. 1368 ; O. M. NO. 540.

SHERLINGS. A.D. 1609. An arable field of about 9 acres amongst five owners.

SHIPHOUSE. A.D. 1609. Belonged to Turner. *See* Sheephouse.

SHIPHOUSE CLOSE. A.D. 1609. Part of Readings.

SHIPHOUSE CLOSE. A.D. 1609. Part of Bradleys. Now Little Shepherds Close.

SHIP ORCHARD. T. M. NO. 293 ; O. M. NO. 438.
A house called " The Old Ship " formerly stood at what is now the village end of the roadway to Sutton. It was, I believe, a public house used by the men who worked the barges up stream, from Ray Mills to Cookham, on their return by the direct road. This portion of the Back Lane was known as the Ship Lane.

SHORFERE. A.D. 1609. Part of Lawrences.

SHORTCROPS LOWER. T. M. NO. 149 ; O. M. NO. 102.

SHORTCROPS UPPER. T. M. NO. 43 ; O. M. NO. 101.

SHORT DOLL. A.D. 1609. Part of Readings.

SHORT DOLL CLOSE. A.D. 1609. Belonged to Turner.

SHORT LAWRENCE. A.D. 1609. Belonged to Page.

SHORTS CROFT. A.D. 1609. A part of Rowborrow.

SHREW. T. M. NO. 1313 ; O. M. NO. 511.
Shaw, shrew, *E.*, from *scearu*, a share or division (Edm.).

SIDENHAM. A.D. 1609. Part of Bullox.

Sid, *B.*, perhaps, *ys*, low-lying, and *yd*, corn land (Edm.). *See* Sydenham Mead.

SIX ACRES, MAIDENHEAD LANE. T. M. NO. 715; O. M. NOS. 324 and 325. See Hall Dore.

SLADES GREAT. T. M. NO. 762; O. M. NO. 155.

SLADES GREAT. T. M. NO. 1203; O. M. NO. 664.

SLADES LITTLE. T. M. NO. 760; O. M. NO. 307.

SLADES LITTLE. T. M. NO. 1195; O. M. NO. 678.

SLADES MEADOW. T. M. NO. 1938; O. M. NO. 22.

SLADES ORCHARD. T. M. NO. 764; O. M. NO. 281.

SLADES SHAW. T. M. NO. 1193; O. M. NO. 679.

SLADES SHAW FURLONG. T. M. NO. 1939; O. M. NO. 22.

SLADES SHOT. Part of Ray Field.

Slaid, sled, *E.*, from *slæd*, open country (Edm.).

SLANDES. A.D. 1527. Robert Hothen does fealty for Slandes (C. C. R.).

SLIPE. T. M. NO. 283; O. M. NO. 356 (part of).

SLIPE. T. M. NO. 1231; O. M. NO. 623.

SLIPE ORCHARD. T. M. NO. 785; O. M. NO. 280.

SLOWGROVE. A.D. 1609. Apportioned between Saracen's head and Bullox.

A.D. 1253. Simon Passelewe excepts, from a grant of one hide of land at Cokcham to William fitz Swayn and Joan his wife, a certain meadow called Slowgrove, which he retains for his life. William and Joan to cut the grass and carry the hay for the said Simon (Feet of Fines).

A.D. 1355. The fishery of Slowgrove is mentioned in the bailiff's account of the Manor of Cookham, and again in the years 1368 and 1465.

Slo, *E.*, from *slog*, a slough (Edm.). Bailey gives

slough, of a wild boar where he wallows in the day-time. *See* Slowgrove.

SLOWGROVE. T. M. NO. 1081 ; O. M. NO. 662. The side next the river is a low-lying swampy meadow intersected with ditches. *See* **Slowgrove.**

SMALL MEADE. A.D. 1609. The northern part of Westmeade, an area of 4¾ acres amongst twelve owners. *See* Small Mead.

A.D. 1471. A hedge lies open at Smalmed (C. C. R.).

SMALL MEADE. T. M. NOS. between 570 and 620 ; O. M. NOS. between 351 and 374.

SMALL MEADE SHOT. T. M. NOS. between 588 and 613 ; O. M. NO. 373.

SMITH CLOSE. A.D. 1609. Belonged to Dorothy Fitzwilliam.

SMYTHMEDE. A.D. 1540. John Butler ought to have a way from his meadow called Smythmede (C. C. R.).

SOANES. A.D. 1609. Arable and woodland belonging to Prentall. Sonnes or essoin land is land for which the owner is excused from an appearance at the Court Baron. *See* Soanes.

SOANES. T. M. NO. 752 ; O. M. NO. 309.

SOMERCLOSE. A.D. 1609. Belonged to Farmer.

SOMERCLOSE. A.D. 1609. Belonged to Turner.

SOMERLEAZE. A.D 1609. Belonged to Sir John Herbert. *See* Summer leaze. T. M. NO. 1806 ; O. M. NO. 13.

SOONS. A.D. 1543. Belonged to Coksetter ; who bequeathed his copie hould named Soons, and his greatest brass pott to his natural son Richard (Cookham Wills).

SOUTER. A.D. 1609. Belonged to Lord Norris.

SOUTHFIELD. A.D. 1609. Belonged to Mattingley.

SOUTH FIELD. T. M. NO. 1020 ; O. M. NO. 663 (part of).

SOUTHEY CLOSE. T. M. NO. 1033 ; O. M. NO. 659.

SOUTHEY, LOWER. A.D. 1609. An arable common field, in area 27 acres, amongst five owners.

> A.D. 1574. Thomas Use bequeaths 5 akers of Barly in Southey (Cookham Wills).
>
> South, *E.*, from *suth*, the south ; ey, *E.*, land surrounded or partly surrounded by water (Edm.).
>
> The two Southeys are nearly surrounded by ditches or running water.

SOUTHEY, LOWER. T. M. NOS. between 1040 and 1156 ; O. M. NOS. 661, 667, 668, 669. An arable common field of 60½ acres, in fifty-seven portions, amongst nine owners.

SOUTHEY, UPPER. A.D. 1609. An arable common field of 119 acres amongst fourteen owners.

SOUTHEY, UPPER. T. M. NOS. between 1024 and 1210 ; O. M. NOS. 661, 663, 669. An arable common field of 87 acres, in forty-nine portions, amongst five owners.

SOUTHIE. A.D. 1609. Reading and Cock held land in Southie.

SOWLLAZE. A.D. 1609. Part of Bullox.

> Sowe, *E.*, from *sawan*, to sow ; leighs, from *lege*, meadow land (Edm.).

SPENCER'S FARM HOMESTEAD. T. M. NO. 1235 ; O. M. NO. 613. Named after a former owner.

> A.D. 1324. Enquiry as to a messuage in Cocham granted to John le Spencer (q. vt.) called Aldebury. (Inq. qd. damn., 18 Ed. 2nd.) This old bury or earthwork lies just below the homestead at Spencer's. *See* North Moor.
>
> Though in later times Spencers and Knight Ellington are treated as the same Manor, yet

II

Spencers must have been a distinct property in the Manor.

A.D. 1356. At a Court held at La Leigh, Henry de Elynton sued John le Spencer for tresspass (C. C. R.).

A.D. 1556. Thomas Lutman, of Cokeham, leaves by his will to his son Roger the half part of his *leese* and *ferme* at Cokeham called Spencers (Cookham Wills). *See* **Ellington.**

SPIKE ORCHARD. T. M. NO. 798 ; O. M. NO. 280.

SPOTS MEAD. T. M. NO. 29 ; O. M. NO. 65. Formerly Reycrofts Coppice.

SPRING CLOSE. *See* Curby Close.

SQUIRES. A.D. 1609. Belonged to Kenton. Named probably from a former owner.

A.D. 1356. At a Court held at La Legh, John le Squyer is one of the afferers (C. C. R.).

A.D. 1394. John Silvester elected Collector for his tenement of Sqyers (C. C. R.). .

A.D. 1505. Alice Bukland bequeaths to Silvester Pecke a tenement called Squyers in Cokeham (Berks Wills).

STERLINGS, or STARLINGS, HOMESTEAD. T. M. NO. 744 ; O. M. NO. 316. Named after Henry, 5th Earl of Sterling. He became possessed of it through his wife, who was the daughter of Sir Edward Hoby, of Bisham, and the widow of her cousin, John Hoby. Lady Sterling is buried at Bisham ; her husband at Binfield. Starlings probably came to the Hobys with the Bisham property, which was acquired by way of exchange with Anne of Cleves, Henry VIII's divorced queen.

STERLINGS GREEN. O. M. NO. 312. The church and churchyard are on a part of this green, which in former days was the site of the parish stocks.

STICH. A.D. 1609. Belonged chiefly to Howden. Stick, Stix, *E.*, from *stig*, a way.

Stich also was a recognised quantity in dealing with eels—twenty-five to the stich—and as the fishery of Cogswell ended just below the Stich this is probably the place where the eels were counted and assorted, either for sale or the payment of rent, which was made in kind.

STICH, THE. T. M. NO. 184 ; O. M. NO. 164.

STONDE, LE. A.D. 1322. Account of fisheries in the water of Le Stonde (Minis. Accts. Exch.).

STONEHOUSE. A.D. 1532. The Prior of Bustleham held of the Lady Anne, Queen of England, a certain tenement in Cokeham called Stonehouse (Aug. Off. $\frac{22}{23}$ Hen. 8th). It is probable that Stonehouse was built by the monks of Bisham, and, if so, this would account for the solidity of the work, and possibly confer on it the name. The walls were pulled down and the materials used for building the church of St. James, Camley Corner, about the year 1850.

STONEHOUSE. T. M. NO. 12 ; O. M. NO. 63.

STONEHOUSE MEADOW. T. M. NO. 11 ; O. M. NO. 63.

STONEY CLOSE. A.D. 1709. John Dodson lets Robert Wilks a close called Stoney Close. Before that **Stoney Croft.** Now Dry Close.

STONEY CROFT. A.D. 1609. Belonged to Cock. *See* Dry Close.

STONEY LEE. A.D. 1609. Part of Bradleys.
Lee, *E.*, from *lege*, meadow land. *See* Stoney Leys.
Would Stoney Ley be a corruption of Stonehouse ? Together with Stonehouse the monks of Bisham held some hollande or hill land.

STONEY LEE, GREAT. A.D. 1609. Part of Bradleys. *See* Leys Stoney.

STONEY LEYS. T. M. NO. 78; O. M. NO. 119. Formerly **Stoney Lee.**

STORTS or STURTS. A.D. 1561. Arthur Babham bequeaths Bare Leaze and Priors Leaze, otherwise called Storts or Sturts (Cookham Wills).

STRAND. A.D. 1609. Belonged to Weldon. *See* Strand Reach.

STRAND FISHERY. A.D. 1609. Belonged to Babham. *See* Strand Water.

STRAND REACH. T. M. NOS. 499 and 524; O. M. NO. 411. *See* **Strand.**

STRAND SWATHE. A.D. 1609. Bullox.

STRAND SWATHE CLOSE. A.D. 1609. Woodyour.

STRAND WATER. T. M. NO. 502; O. M. NO. 378.

STRANGES. T. M. NO. 1480; O. M. NO. 760.
Strang, *E.*, a corruption of *steng*, a pole (Edm.).

STROND. A.D. 1609. Weldon.

STRONDE CLOSE. A.D. 1650. John Plummer paid 2*s.* rent for Stronde Close (Commonwealth Survey).

STUBBINGS. Part of the park. T. M. NO. 1498.
From *stub*, *D.*, stump of a tree, and *ing*, a meadow (Edm.).

SUMMERHOUSE MEADOW. T. M. NO. 22; O. M. NO. 64.
Formerly called Beechwood Temple.

SUMMER LEAZE. T. M. NO. 1806; O. M. NO. 13.

SUMMER LEYS SHOT. T. M. NOS. between 1998 and 2007; O. M. NO. 41.

SUTTON. A.D. 1609. A common arable field of 183 acres amongst twenty owners. Sut, *E.*, from *suth*, south, and tun, *E.*, a settlement. *See* Sutton Field.

SUTTON FIELD. T. M. NOS. between 410 and 567;
  O. M. NOS. between 446 and 487. Area 177 acres,
  in ninety-two portions, amongst thirteen owners.

SWEDE MEADE. A.D. 1609. Belonged to Smith.
  Swad, *E.*, from *swath*, a path (Edm.).

SWINESEAD HOMESTEAD. T. M. NO. 98; O. M.
  NO. 130.

SWINESHEAD STILE. A.D. 1609.
  A.D. 1470. A gate lies open at Swineshead (C. C. R.).
    Swin, *E.*, swine; head, either heigh, from *heah*,
    high or hat, *E.*, from *haeth*, a heath.
    Swineshead was probably an open place in the
    woods where the swineherd collected his charge.
    This custom of turning the pigs out to common
    pasture continued in Cookham village up to fifty or
    sixty years ago. Excepting in winter time, the pigs
    of the inhabitants, often a very considerable drove,
    were sent across the brook every morning into Odney
    Common. In the afternoon they returned to their
    several homes of their own accord.

SYDENHAM MEAD. T. M. NO. 1048; O. M. NO. 504.
  See **Sidenham.**

SYDENHAM MEAD FURLONG. T. M. NO. 1039;
  O. M. NO. 661. Part of Upper Southey.

TARRY STONE. A stone 3½ ft. high, by 4 ft. long,
  and 2½ ft. thick. This formerly stood in Cookham
  village, about two feet from Dodson's fence, where the
  roads parted to the church and the ferry. It is now
  in the Mill Garden at Cookham, where it was removed
  by the late George Venables when he was church-
  warden. This stone was formerly known as *Cookham Stone.*
  A.D. 1506. The tithing man presents that the Warrener
    ought to hold sports at Cookham Stone on the day
    of Assumption; and he has not done so (C. C. R.).
    The stone was originally a boundary stone to the

property of the Abbot of Cirencester, whose house was close by, as is shown in the will of John Luffenham, A.D. 1423.

Similar boundary stones are yet to be found in the neighbourhood, as in West Mead (at the south-east corner of the piece No. 623 in the Tithe Map), another at south-west corner of No. 624, and another at the south-west corner of No. 625.

TARR BUCK
TARR COCKMARSH
TARR GREAT
TARR HORNEYARDE
TARR LITTLE
TARR LONGMEAD   Islands in the river Thames.
TARR OOZIE
TARR PEACOCK
TARR ROUND
TARR WILLOWS

TERRIS CLOSE. A.D. 1609. Belonged to Hamerton.

A.D. 1451. William Norreys held Terrys in Cokeham.

TERRORS GROVE. A.D. 1609. Belonged to Woodyour. *See* Terrys Coppice.

TERRORS GROVE ARABLE. A.D. 1609. Belonged to Woodyour. *See* Terrys, Great and Little.

TERRYS COPPICE. T. M. NO. 100 ; O. M. NO. 132. The foundations of a considerable range of buildings exist here.

TERRYS, GREAT. T. M. NO. 103 ; O. M. NO. 162.

TERRYS, LITTLE. T. M. NO. 101 ; O. M. NO. 163.

TERRYS, LITTLE. T. M. NO. 46 ; O. M. NO. 133.

THICKET, MAIDENHEAD. T. M. NO. 1497 ; O. M. NO. 773. An open common of pasturage for freeholders of the Manor ; in area about 368 acres.

In the survey of A.D. 1609 it appears as Great Thicket 200 acres, Little Thicket 100 acres.

A.D. 1321. Inquiry at Elynton as to that tenants, and

no others, have and take housebote, and heybote, and fuel &c., on the Thickette (Inq. qd. damn., 14 Ed. 2nd).

A.D. 1390. Le Thickette appears in the enrolment of a deed of Thomas White (C. C. R.).

Ette or atte, meaning a place. Thickette indicates a place thickly covered by undergrowth.

There is an old earthwork encampment on the Thicket near to Stubbing's house.

THREE CLOSES. T. M. NO. 27 ; O. M. NO. 66.
Formerly **Little Middons.**

THUMPS. T. M. NO. 825 ; O. M. NO. 108.
Probably a corruption either of thrump, *E.*, from *thrym*, a meeting place, or of tump, *B.*, from *twmp*, a small round hill (Edm.).

TILE COPPICE. T. M. NO. 1306 ; O. M. NOS. 267 and 393.

TILERS COPPICE. T. M. NO. 52 ; O. M. NO. 88.

TILL CLOSE. A.D. 1609. Part of Harwoods. *See* Bigfrith Shaw.

TOTEHILL STYLE. A.D. 1488. A hedge ruinous at Totehill Style (C. C. R.).

TOWNSEN CLOSE. T. M. NO. 18 ; O. M. NO. 69.

TOWNSEN WOOD. T. M. NO. 19 ; O. M. NO. 68.

TRYNDLE ACRE. A.D. 1503. An acre in Wellhouse-field, given by William Brice, called *Tryndle Acre*, for a light in Maidenhead Chapel (Nicholls).

Trental, an office for the dead of thirty masses.

TUCKS ORCHARD. T. M. NO. 76 ; O. M. NO. 116.
Name of former occupant.

TUGGINS LANE. A.D. 1609. Comes in the boundary of Cookham parish (Survey, A.D. 1609).

TUGWOOD COMMON. O. M. NO. 28. Lies at the north end of Grubwood Lane. The Tugwoods occupied a cottage on T. M. NOS. 843, 844 ; O. M. NO. 45. It was an old parish house, since pulled· down by J. Darby.

TULEYS, GREAT. T. M. NO. 51 ; O. M. NO. 88.

TULEYS, LITTLE. T. M. NO. 41 ; O. M. NO. 88.
Tuleys is probably the same as Tilers.

TURNERS CLOSE. T. M. NO. 53 ; O. M. NO. 88.

TURNERS MEAD. A.D. 1633. A parcel of land near Cookham Lock called Turners Mead (Ex. Com. Enq., 9 Charles 1st).

TYNTER EIOTT. An island in the Thames.

UPPER BROAD MEAD. T. M. NO. 35 ; O. M. NO. 7.

LOWER BROAD MEAD. T. M. NO. 36 ; O. M. NO. 6.

UPPER FIELD, MAIDENHEAD. A.D. 1609. An open arable field of 167 acres amongst 16 owners. *See* Maidenhead Upper Field.

UPPER MEADOW. T. M. NO. 1787 ; O. M. NO. 18.

VANBEDD. A.D. 1633. A place near Salisbury Pitt called Vanbedd (Ex. Com. Enq., 9 Charles 1st).

VICCARIDGE BERRY. A.D. 1685. A messuage in Cookham let to Thomas Smith was bounded on the north by the Viccaridge Berry (private doc.).

WARNERS HILL. From the east end of Hardings Green to the Dean. On the west side of O. M. NO. 281. In Bingley's Map of the Common it is named Walnuts Hill. It abuts on Great Slades, out of which, in the old French war, more than £200 worth of walnut timber was said to have been sold for musket stocks.

WARPOLE FURLONG. T. M. NO. 505 ; O. M. NO. 487.
A part of Sutton Field.
Whapple-way, a way where a cart and horses cannot pass, but horses only (Bailey).

WARPOLE GORE. A.D. 1656. Land in Sutton bounded by Warpole Gore (private doc.).

WASDELL SHOT. LOWER, MIDDLE, and UPPER. T. M. NOS. 1943, &c.; O. M. NOS. 218, 220, 221. Part of Ray Field. Was, *E.*, *waes*, water; dell, a pit.

WATERBUTTS MEADOW. T. M. NOS. between 1096 and 1124; O. M. NOS. 661 to 669.

WATERDELLS. A.D. 1609. John Sharpe had land in Pound Field, near Waterdells.

WATERLOO CLOSE. T. M. NO. 579; O. M. NO. 368.

WATERY BUTTS. T. M. NO. 1083; O. M. Now a part of Bartle Mead.

WELL CLOSE. A.D. 1609. Part of Pinkneys.

WELL COPPICE. T. M. NO. 1385; O. M. NO. 768.

WELLHOUSE FIELD. A.D. 1609. An open arable field of ninety acres amongst fifteen owners.

The name Wellhouse is a corruption of Wealas. "The Saxons and Angles, not content with having dispossessed the children of the soil of their lands, called them Wealas, *i. e.* strangers" (Taylor, 'Names and Places').

Wellhouse Field would have been a Romano-British settlement, afterwards appropriated by the Saxons, and the fortifications in North Moor may have been made for its protection. The old Roman way, traceable from Braywick to the Ham settlement, passed through Wellhouse Field. Hurstreet or Horstreet also led from it. The land enclosed by the highway from the " Harrow" public-house to Spencers, thence to the Furze Platt, thence to the Harrow Lane, thence to the " Harrow," an area of 102 acres, was probably the extent of the old settlement.

WELLHOUSE FIELD. T. M. NOS. 1760 to 1781; O. M. NOS. 640 and 641.

An area of only 19½ acres, in seventeen portions, amongst eight owners.

WELLHOUSE FIELD LANE. A.D. 1583. Appears in the will of Thomas Osbourne. It is now the Harrow Lane.

WELLONDES. A.D. 1469. Lands called Wellondes (C. C. R.).

WESSENHAM LANE. A.D. 1410. A watercourse in Wessenham Lane (C. C. R.).
Wessing, *E.*, from *wæs*, water, indicating a moist or wet place.

WESSONS HILL. The hill facing north by Ragaback Close.

WESTMEADE. A.D. 1609. An open common meadow of 107 acres, amongst twenty owners. It extended from Cookham Moor to North Town Moor. West acquired possibly from Wäste or vast, the great meadow. *See* Westmead.

WESTMEAD. T. M. NOS. 569 to 629, and 1212 and 1253 ; O. M. NOS. between 374 and 416. An area of 97 acres, in fifty-six portions, amongst seventeen owners.

It was severalled for hay and afterwards was common for pasturage to the owners, who were not restricted, as in the other meadows (the Marsh, Bartlemead, &c.), to the size of their holdings, but might turn out to pasture as much stock as they could winter, following the rule with the freeholders of the manor, on the open commons ; and so perhaps West may mean Waste or common meadow.

WETTONS MEADOW. T. M. NO. 2314 ; O. M. NO. 195.

WETTONS MOOR. T. M. NO. 2317 ; O. M. NO. 195. Name from a former owner.

WHIRLPOOL SHOT. T. M. NO. 665 ; O. M. NO. 365. Part of Ham Field.
Probably a corruption of Warpole.

WHITE PLACE. A.D. 1609. Part of Bullox.

White Place, or the name which originated it, is probably an earlier one than that of Bullox or Bullocks. It may have been acquired from the white chalk hill under which it lay, Whit, *E.*, from *kwit*, white (Edm.), or it may have been acquired from some Saxon or Danish personage. Saxon names with the prefix Wiht were common, and White Place joins Babbaham, which again joins Odin Eye. *See* White Place Mansion.

In Minister's Accounts, 44th year of Edward the 3rd, appears an amount of rent paid for two acres of land lying in Southey by Richard le Whyte; who probably derived his name from the locality, as did Gilbert Odeney, who in the same account pays rent for six acres of land sometime Andrew Smythe's.

WHITE PLACE MANSION. T. M. NO. 467; O. M. NO. 496.

WHITE PLACE LAWN. T. M. NO. 469; O. M. NO. 498. *See* **White Place.**

WHITTLEA. T. M. NO. 460; O. M. NO. 495.

WHITELEY CLOSE. A.D. 1609. Bullox. *See* Whittlea.

WHITELEY. GATE. A.D. 1609. Bullox. *See* Whittlea.

WHITELEY GREAT HARE WARREN. T. M. NO. 405; O. M. NO. 479.

WIDBROOK CLOSE. T. M. NO. 491; O. M. NO. 487.

WIDBROOK. A.D. 1609. A pasture ground of 50 acres, common to the inhabitants of Cookham.
A.D. 1392. William de Elynton held a pasture of Cokeham called Whitbrok (Kerry).
The derivation of the name is probably the same as that of White Place.

WIDBROOK COMMON. T. M. NO. 475 ; O. M. NOS. 501, 502. An area of 67 acres, common to the inhabitants of Cookham.

WIDBROOK FURLONG. T. M. NO. 1004 ; O. M. NO. 663. Part of Upper Southey.

WINCHMEADE. A.D. 1609. Part of Bullox.
Winch, *E.*, from *wincel*, a corner or nook (Edm.).

WINCHMEADE SWATHE. A.D. 1609. In Bartle-meade.

WINDMILL COPPICE, or SHEPHERD'S COP-PICE. A.D. 1609. Part of Harwoods. *See* Windmill Shaw.

WINDMILL FIELD. A.D. 1609. Part of Harwoods.
Win, *E.*, victory (Edm.). Windmill Field adjoins Ham Field, and may have been the spot where a successful defence of the settlement was made. Possibly the pits in Windmill Shaw have some bearing on this. The situation is not one that would have been chosen for the site of a windmill, and windmills were as little likely then, as now, to have been used here, with an abundance of water power so near. *See* Windmill Field.

WINDMILL FIELD. T. M. NO. 983 ; O. M. NO. 400.

WINDMILL FIELD. T. M. NO. 1655 ; O. M. NO. 99 (part of).

WINDMILL SHAW. T. M. NOS. 981 and 982 ; O. M. NOS. 382 and 399.
In the small portion of this wood belonging to Woodmancutts are four circular or slightly oval pits of varying sizes and depths. They appear to have been made with a purpose and not to be holes left after digging for earthy materials.

WINTER HILL HOMESTEAD. T. M. NO. 62 ; O. M. NO. 82.
The site of an ancient homestead. *See* **Dyall Close.**

Winter, *E.*, the British *gwent*, bright, became the Roman *venta*, and Saxonised naturally into Winter (Edm.).

Winter Hill, from its position catching the early morning sun, would be *the bright hill.*

In Kerry's Bray the name Windounhull occurs in connection with Boyne Hill farm, which was a part of the Manor of Ives, which manor at one time belonged to Queen Anne (of Cleves), and the farm was in the tenure of the Monks of Bisham. Now the Prior of Bustleham Monastery, Berks, according to the Augmentation Office Surveys, $\frac{23}{32}$ Henry the 8th, held of the Lady Anne, Queen of England, a certain tenement in Cokeham called Stonehouse (*see* **Stonehouse**) and certain lands in Cokeham called Hollande, or the hill land, and possibly the name Windounhull may have become mixed up, or it may have been applied both to Boyne Hill and Winter Hill.

WIX PIGHTLE. T. M. NO. 70 ; O. M. NO. 116. Named after a former occupier.

WOODMANCUTTS. A.D. 1609. Belonged to the College of Eton.

A.D. 1545. Thomas to dwell in the ferme called Woodmancotes (Will of William Kimber).

WOODMANCUTTS CLOSES. A.D. 1609. Ten closes belonging to Woodmancutts.

WOODMANCUTTS STILE. A.D. 1609. Woodyour had land at Woodmancutts Stile.

WOODMANCUTTS FARM HOMESTEAD. T. M. NO. 730 ; O. M. NO. 230.

WOODWARDS. *See* Godfreys.

WOOLHOUSE FIELD. A.D. 1609. Woreston had land in Woolhouse Field.

WOOVEYS. A.D. 1731. Terry rented Wooveys (private doc.). *See* Oveys.

WORKHOUSE MEADOW. T. M. NO. 2014; O. M. NO. 87. *See* Latimore House.

WORKHOUSE SHOT. T. M. NO. 2081; O. M. NO. 75. A part of Middle Maidenhead Field.

WORTH END GATE. A.D. 1574. By Worth end gate as you go to Beeching Grove (Will of Thos. Use).

WORTHY, LOWER. T. M. NO. 1734; O. M. NO. 610.

WORTHY, UPPER. T. M. NO. 1733; O. M. NO. 609.

WYNCHES. Mentioned in the will of Alice Bukland, A.D. 1505. The name, probably, of a former owner.

WYNSLOWE. A.D. 1481. A water-course called Wynslowe (C. C. R.).

WYSSES. A.D. 1489. Lands and tenements called Wysses (C. C. R.).

YANKS. T. M. NO. 827; O. M. NO. 27.

Yax, *E.*, from *æc*, an oak, or *æsce*, an axe indicating a clearing in the forest (Edm.). *See* **Farthings.**

LONDON : PRINTED BY ADLARD AND SON, BARTHOLOMEW CLOSE, E.C., AND 20, HANOVER SQUARE, W.

www.ingramcontent.com/pod-product-compliance
Lightning Source LLC
Chambersburg PA
CBHW021411090426
42742CB00009B/1103